LIFE IN TH

1st Standard Translation Book in Urdu Language

Citizenship Study Guide

1st Edition 2009

Translated and edited by
Rehan Afzal

Chapter 2,3,4,5 & 6

Published with the permission of Her Majesty's Stationary Office

PSI (on behalf of Home Office) Licence no: C 2009000024

Visit us online at www.authorsonline.co.uk

A Bright Pen Book

Copyright Rehan Afzal © 2009

Cover design by Rehan Afzal ©

All rights reserved. No part of this publication may be reproduced, stored in a retrieval system, or transmitted in any form or by any means, electronic, mechanical, photocopy, recording or otherwise, without prior written permission of the copyright owner. Nor can it be circulated in any form of binding or cover other than that in which it is published and without similar condition including this condition being imposed on a subsequent purchaser.

ISBN 978-07552-1156-2

Authors OnLine Ltd
19 The Cinques
Gamlingay, Sandy
Bedfordshire SG19 3NU
England

This book is also available in e-book format, details of which are available at www.authorsonline.co.uk

لائف ان دایو کے بک ان لوگوں کیلئے بنائی گئی ہے جو برطانیہ میں مستقل رہائش رکھنا چاہتے ہیں اور اس مقصد کیلئے نیشنیلٹی لینا چاہتے ہیں یا پھر وہ ان ڈیفینیٹ سٹے اپلائی کرنا چاہتے ہیں۔ لائف ان دایو کے ٹیسٹ پاس کر کے آپ یہ ثابت کر سکتے ہیں کہ آپ کو انگریزی زبان میں مہارت حاصل ہے۔ کچھ لوگ جو لائف ان دایو کا ٹیسٹ پاس نہیں کر سکتے وہ ایک اور طرح کا ٹیسٹ جسے ESOL کہتے ہیں جس کا مخفف یہ ہے (دوسری زبان بولنے والوں کیلئے انگلش کا کورس English to the Speaker of Other Languges) پاس کر سکتے ہیں۔ لیکن اس وقت ہوم آفس نے بے شمار ادارے جو کہ ایک دن کا یا ایک ہفتے کا کورس کروا کر سرٹیفیکیٹ بیچتے ہیں بند کر دیئے ہیں اور ان کا سرٹیفیکیٹ ہوم آفس سے ریفیوز ہو جاتا ہے۔ بد قسمتی سے اچھے برے کئی اداروں کا سرٹیفیکیٹ ریفیوز ہو جاتا ہے اس لئے لائف ان دایو کے بک خرید کر ٹیسٹ خود کریں پاس کریں اور اپنا قیمتی سرمایہ بچائیں۔ ایسول کورس صرف اسی صورت میں کریں جب آپ کم از کم دو یا چار مہینے کی تیاری کر کے تھوڑی بہت انگلش بولنا سیکھ لیتے ہیں یا پھر انگلش ٹیسٹ بغیر کسی کی مدد کے پاس کر سکیں۔ آپ ہمیں فون کر کے پتہ کروا سکتے ہیں کہ کونسے ادارے ہیں جو ESOL کورس دو یا چار ماہ میں کسی کی نگرانی میں اور ریجنل ٹیسٹ کرواتے ہیں

لائف ان دایو کے بک (شہریت کی طرف سفر) کا ترجمہ آسان اردو میں کیا گیا ہے تا کہ کم پڑھے لکھے افراد بھی آسانی سے سمجھ سکیں اور آن لائن ٹیسٹ میں پہلی مرتبہ کامیاب ہوں۔ لائف ان دایو کے بک کا لفظ بالفظ ترجمہ کرنے کے بجائے صرف اہم جملے اور امتحان میں لازمی آنے والے ٹاپک کا ترجمہ کیا گیا ہے تا کہ بہت جلدی اور کم وقت میں با مقصد تیاری کر سکیں اور اپنا قیمتی وقت بچائیں اور بلا وجہ فضول سوال جو کہ امتحان میں نہیں آتے ان کو یاد کرنے کی پریشانی سے بچیں۔ اس بک میں وہ سب کچھ شامل ہے جو امتحان پاس کرنے کیلئے ضروری ہے۔

لائف ان دایو کے ٹیسٹ کا کل وقت 45 منٹ ہوتا ہے اور 24 سوالوں پر مشتمل ہے اور پاس کرنے کے لئے 18 سوال ٹھیک ہونے چاہئیں جو کہ 75% بنتا ہے۔ اس کا مطلب ہے کہ آپ صرف اور صرف 6 غلطیاں کر سکتے ہیں یہ آن لائن ٹیسٹ ہوتا ہے اور ٹیسٹ کے ختم ہوتے ہی آپ کو رزلٹ بتا دیتے ہیں۔ اس وقت ٹیسٹ کی فی

34.00 پاؤنڈ ہے۔ لائف ان دا یو کے کا ٹیسٹ پانچ ابواب میں سے آتا ہے یعنی چیپٹر 2 سے لے کر چیپٹر 6 تک۔ مختلف لوگوں کا مختلف طریقہ کا رہوتا ہے یاد کرنے کا اور کچھ لوگوں کا اچھا حافظہ ہوتا ہے اور وہ جلدی امتحان پاس کر لیتے ہیں۔ یہی وجہ ہے کہ کچھ لوگ جنہوں نے کبھی سکول نہیں دیکھا وہ بھی لائف ان دا یو کے پاس کر لیتے ہیں۔

لائف ان دا یو کے کا امتحان پاس کرنے کیلئے تقریباً 300 سوالات آپ کو آنے چاہئیں۔ امید ہے کہ یہ بک چھپنے سے پہلے پہلے سوالات اس بک میں شامل کر دئے جائیں گے ورنہ آپ کو سوالات یا تیاری کیلئے الگ کتاب لینی پڑ گی۔ لائف ان دا یو کے کی تیاری سی ڈی میں بھی کی جاسکتی ہے اور آپ ہم سے لائف ان دا یو کے کی اردو سی ڈی بھی خرید سکتے ہیں۔

یہ بک پہلی مرتبہ پرنٹ کی جا رہی ہے اور آپ کی رائے اور مشورے سے جو بھی تجاویز ہم تک پہنچیں گی اگلی مرتبہ اور بہتر انداز میں بک چھاپنے کی کوشش کرینگے۔ بہت جلد نیا ایڈیشن چھاپا جائیگا اور اگر کسی کو یہ بک کہیں سے نہ مل رہی ہو تو پلیز فون کر کے یا ای میل کر کے منگوا سکتے ہیں اور یہ بک چھپنے کے فوراً بعد ہی نیا ایڈیشن جو کہ آپ کی رائے سے اور بہتر ہو جائے گا آپ کیلئے دستیاب ہو گا۔ email:lifeintheuktest@hotmail.co.uk
فون 07973863002, 07815606143

Translated & Edited by:
Rehan Afzal

کتاب ملنے کا پتہ
89-90 نارتھ گیٹ ہاؤس ہائی سٹریٹ ڈڈلی (ویسٹ مڈلینڈ) DY1 1QP
نوٹ: لائف ان دا یو کے بک کا ترجمہ کاپی رائٹ ہے اور ہوم آفس سے لائسنس یافتہ ہے

پی ایس آئی PSI (Home Office) Licence No: C2009000024

فہرست

I	لائف ان دی یو کے کی ٹیسٹ کی معلومات
1	چیپٹر 2 بدلتی سوسائٹی
15	چیپٹر 3 یو کے آج
27	چیپٹر 4 برطانیہ کا طرزِ حکومت
49	چیپٹر 5 روزمرہ کی ضروریات
75	چیپٹر 6 روزگار
90	برٹش ہسٹری 1530 سے 2006 تک
92	پریکٹس ایگزیم

HOW TO ANSWER QUESTIONS
These pages helps you to find your way around the Life in the UK Test and gives you the chance to practice answering some simple questions. These questions are just for fun, but will help you understand how to answer questions on a computer. You will also find out some important information about the test.

PERSONAL DETAILS
Before you take the test at your test centre, the test supervisor will check your photographic ID to confirm your identity. The test supervisor also needs to record some of your personal details such as your name, date of birth and postcode.

TEST INFORMATION
You will have 45 minutes to answer 24 questions. This gives you plenty of time to choose your answers and check them again before the end. You can have longer to take the test if you have particular needs. Please ask your test centre about this when you book your test. Some of the test questions will be relevant to the part of the UK you live in - England, Scotland, Wales or Northern Ireland. You will not be able to look for answers in the 'Life in the United Kingdom' handbook during the test.

PRACTICE TEST
Once your details have been recorded, you are logged in to the test computer. You then have the option to complete a Practice Test before you begin the Life in the UK Test. We recommend that you complete the Practice Test before moving on to the real test.

TEST SCREEN - A
This is what the Life in the UK Test will look like. The boxes along the top let you move between questions. Each of the 24 boxes represents one question. You can move quickly to any question by simply selecting a box with your mouse or keyboard.

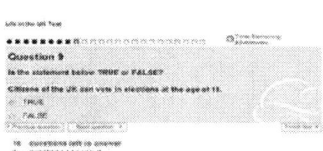

TEST SCREEN - B

A white box means that you have not yet visited a question. A white box with a blue outline means you have visited a question but not answered it.
A blue box means you have answered a question. Using the boxes to move around the test lets you visit questions first and return to them later. This is especially useful when you're not sure what the answer to a question is, or if you want to change a previous answer.

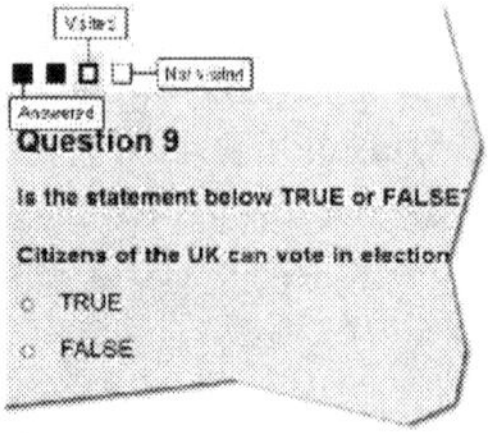

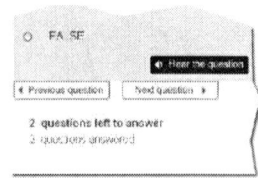

TEST SCREEN - C

Selecting Hear the question turns on the audio. This reads out the question to you. There may be a slight delay before you can hear the question.
Selecting Next question takes you to the next question in the test. Selecting Previous question returns you to the previous question in the test. Questions left to answer tells you how many questions you have left to answer. Questions answered tells you how many you have answered.

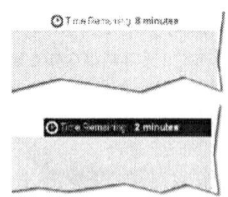

TEST SCREEN - D

The timer counts down your time from when you start the test. It is always there, so you know how much time you have left. Halfway through the test time, you will get a time alert. You will get two more time alerts: ten and two minutes before the test ends.

QUESTION TYPES

The test contains four different types of question. You will now have the chance to practise answering each type of question. These aren't real test questions, but they show you how the real test works.

SHORTCUT KEYS - 1

There are some keyboard shortcuts available which you can use to answer questions in the test. You can use these shortcuts instead of or as well as the commands you learn in Keyboard or even if you normally use a mouse.

SHORTCUT KEYS - 2
Answering questions
To select the first answer, press the number 1.
To select the second answer, press the number 2.
To select the third answer, press the number 3.
To select the fourth answer, press the number 4.
To deselect an answer, press the relevant number key again.

SHORTCUT KEYS - 3
Other shortcuts
To move to the next question, select N. To move to the previous question, select P. To hear the question, select H. To finish the test, select F.

SELECTING ANSWERS
When you move to an answer, the area around it turns grey. This means the answer is active and you can select it. If you are using a mouse, your pointer arrow will also change to a pointer finger.
Once you select an answer, the area around it turns white. If you have selected a radio button, a dot will also appear in the circle. If you have selected a tick box, a tick will appear in the box.

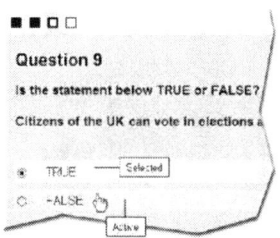

QUESTION PRACTICE - 1
The first type of question involves selecting one correct answer from four options.
Select the correct answer.
Remember, radio buttons deselect automatically when you select another answer. Your selected answer will have a white area around it and a dot in the circle. Remember, this isn't a real test question.
Where is the Prime Minister's official home in London?
Downing Street   Parliament Square   Richmond Terrace   Whitehall Place
(The correct answer is Downing Street.)

> Where is the Prime Minister's official home in London?
> • Downing Street
> • Parliament Square
> • Richmond Terrace
> • Whitehall Place
> (The correct answer is Downing Street.)

QUESTION PRACTICE - 2
The next type of question involves deciding whether a statement is true or false.
Select the correct answer.
Your selected answer will have a white area around it and a dot in the circle. Remember, this isn't a real test question. Is the statement below TRUE or FALSE?
Citizens of the UK can vote in elections at the age of 18.   TRUE   FALSE
(The correct answer is TRUE.)

> Is the statement below TRUE or FALSE?
> Citizens of the UK can vote in elections at the age of 18.
> • TRUE
> • FALSE
> (The correct answer is TRUE.)

Introduction

QUESTION PRACTICE - 3
The next question type involves selecting two correct answers from four options. You should not select more or fewer answers than this!
Select the correct answers.
Remember, you need to select a tick box again to deselect it.
Your selected answers will have white areas around them and ticks in the boxes.
Remember, this isn't a real test question.
Which TWO places can you go to if you need a National Insurance number?
Department for Education and Skills   Home Office   Jobcentre Plus   Social security office
(The correct answers are Jobcentre Plus and Social security office.)

> Which TWO places can you go to if you need a National Insurance number?
>
> Department for Education and Skills
> Home Office
> Jobcentre Plus
> Social security office
>
> (The correct answers are Jobcentre Plus and Social security office.)

QUESTION PRACTICE - 4
The last question type involves selecting which one of two statements you think is correct.
Select the correct answer.
Your selected answer will have a white area around it and a dot in the circle. Remember, this isn't a real test question. Which of these statements is correct?
Scottish bank notes are valid in all parts of the UK. Scottish bank notes are valid only in Scotland.
(The first statement is the correct answer.)

> Which of these statements is correct?
>
> Scottish bank notes are valid in all parts of the UK.
>
> Scottish bank notes are valid only in Scotland.
>
> (The first statement is the correct answer.)

END OF PRACTICE
Well done. You have learned all the skills you need to answer the four types of question in the test. Now the only thing you have to think about is selecting the correct answers!

ENDING THE TEST - 1
The Finish test button ends the test.
You select Finish test when you have completed all 24 questions. If you run out of time, your test will end automatically. You will not be allowed to finish your current question. Don't worry if you select Finish test by mistake; you will be asked to confirm your decision. Remember: none of your answers are final until you select Finish test and confirm your decision.

ENDING THE TEST - 2
Your test results will not be displayed on screen at the end of the test. You will find out your results when the test session has finished. The test supervisor will tell you whether or not you have passed.

IV

Migration to Britain

برطانیہ میں آمد

In the distant past, invaders came to Britain, seized land and stayed. More recently, people come to Britain to find safety, jobs and a better life.

پہلے پہلے لوگ قبضہ کرنے آتے تھے اور یہیں رہ جاتے تھے۔ ابھی لوگ محفوظ جگہ نوکری اور بہتر زندگی کی تلاش میں آتے ہیں

In the 16th and 18th centuries, Huguenots (French Protestants) came to Britain to escape religious persecution in France

سولہویں اور اٹھارویں صدی میں یوگنٹس (فرانسیسی احتجاج) مذہبی جنگ سے بھاگ کر برطانیہ آئے

In the mid-1840s there was a terrible famine in Ireland and many Irish people migrated to Britain

آئرلینڈ میں شدید قحط آیا اور بہت سے آئرش برطانیہ آئے۔

Many Irish men became labourers and helped to build canals and railways across Britain

بہت سے آئرش مزدور بن گئے اور نہریں بنائیں اور ریلوے بنایا۔

From 1880 to 1910, a large number of Jewish people came to Britain to escape racist attacks (called 'pogroms') in what was then called the Russian Empire from the countries now called Poland, Ukrain and Belarus

1880 سے 1990 تک بہت سے جیوش نسلی فسادات (پوگرم) سے بھاگ کر برطانیہ گئے۔ یہ ممالک روس کے پاس تھے۔

After the Second World War (1939-45), there was a huge task of rebuilding Britain.

دوسری جنگ کے بعد برطانیہ کی تعمیر کا بہت بڑا کام تھا۔

the British government encouraged workers from Ireland and other parts of Europe to come to the UK to help with the reconstruction.

Chapter 2   A Changing Society

1

Chapter 2

برطانیہ نے آئرلینڈ اور یورپ سے یو کے کی تعمیر کیلئے لوگ بلائے۔

In 1948, people from the West Indies were also invited to come and work.

1948 میں ویسٹ انڈیز سے بھی کام کیلئے لوگوں کو بلایا۔

During the 1950s, there was still a shortage of labour in the UK.

1950 میں بھی یو کے میں مزدوروں کی کمی تھی۔

The UK encouraged immigration in the 1950s for economic reasons

1950 میں معاشی وجہ سے امیگریشن کھولی۔

Centers were set up in the West Indies to recruit people to drive buses. Textile and engineering firms from the north of England and the Midlands sent agents to India and Pakistan to find workers.

بس چلانے کیلئے ویسٹ انڈیز میں کام دینے کیلئے سینٹر بنایا۔ مڈلینڈ نے ٹیکسٹائل اور انجینرنگ کیلئے ایجنٹ انڈیا اور پاکستان بھیجے۔

For about 25 years people has been coming, people from the West Indies, India, Pakistan, and later Bangladesh, traveled to work and settle in Britain.

25 سال تک لوگ ویسٹ انڈیز، انڈیا، پاکستان اور بنگلہ دیش سے یو کے آتے ہی رہے۔

The number of people migrating from these areas fell in the late 1960s because the government passed new laws to restrict immigration to Britain.

1960 میں یو کے نے پابندی لگائی جسکی وجہ سے ان علاقوں سے لوگ آنے کم ہو گئے

Although immigrants from 'old' Commonwealth countries such as Australia New Zealand and Canada did not have to face such strict controls

البتہ آسٹریلیا نیوزی لینڈ اور کینڈا کو پابندی کا سامنا نہ کرنا پڑا

During this time, however, Britain did admit 28,000 people of Indian origin who had been forced to leave Uganda - and 22,000 refugees from South East Asia.

---

*Key Points To Remember in Chapter 2
*Huguenots are French Protestants who came from France *Pogroms are racist attacks on Jewish people in 1880-1910 *Suffragettes are those women who demonstrated for greater rights e.g. right of vote

اس دوران 28000 انڈین مقامی جو یوگنڈا سے نکالے گئے تھے اور 22000 مہاجر جو ساؤتھ ایسٹ ایشیا سے نکالے تھے انہیں برطانیہ نے پناہ دی۔

In the 1980s the largest immigrant groups came from the United States, Australia, South Africa, and New Zealand

1980 میں سب سے بڑا گروپ یو ایس اے، آسٹریلیا، اور نیوزی لینڈ سے آیا۔

In the early 1990s, groups of people from the former Soviet Union came to Britain look a safer way of life.

1990 کے شروعات میں سویت یونین کے گروپ برطانیہ بہتر زندگی کیلئے آئے

Since 1994 there has been a global rise and in mass migration for both political and economic reasons.

1994 سے پوری دنیا سے ہی لوگ سیاسی اور معاشی وجہ سے برطانیہ آئے ہیں۔

Chapter 2 A Changing Society

THE CHANGING ROLE OF WOMEN

عورتوں کا بدلتا ہوا رول

Women in Britain had fewer rights than men. Until 1857, a married woman had no right to divorce her husband.

مردوں کی نسبت عورتوں کو کم حقوق حاصل ہیں۔

Until 1882, when a woman got married, her earnings, property and money automatically belonged to her husband.

1882 سے پہلے جب عورت کی شادی ہوتی تھی تو اس کی تنخواہ جائداد اور پیسہ خود بخود شوہر کا ہو جاتا تھا۔

In the late 19th and early 20th centuries, an increasing number of women campaigned and demonstrated for greater rights and, in particular, the right to vote. They became known as 'Suffragettes'.

*Children under 19 year of age are 15 million children i.e. 25% of UK population *Children are at work at one time are 2 million * 3/4 (Third fourth) or 75% women at the school age are in paid work

Chapter 2

انیسویں اور بیسویں صدی میں کافی تعداد میں عورتوں نے اپنے حقوق کیلئے مظاہرے کئے اور تحریک چلائی خاص طور پر ووٹ کا حق۔ یہ لوگ سفراگیٹس کے نام سے مشہور ہو گئے

These protests decreased during the First World War because women joined in the war effort and therefore did a much greater variety of work than they had before.

یہ مظاہرے پہلی جنگ کے دوران کم ہو گئے کیونکہ عورتوں نے بڑی تعداد میں جنگ میں حصہ لیا اور بہت کام کیا۔

When the First World War ended in 1918, women over the age of 30 were only given the right to vote and to stand for election to Parliament.

جب 1918 میں پہلی جنگ ختم ہوئی تو عورتوں کو تیس سال کی عمر میں پہلی مرتبہ ووٹ دینے کا حق ملا۔

It was not until 1928 when women won the right to vote at 21, the same age as men.

1928 میں عورتوں کو 21 سال کی عمر میں سیم مردوں کی طرح ووٹ دینے کا حق ملا۔

Women still faced discrimination in the workplace. For example, it was quite common for employers to ask women to leave their jobs when they got married.

خواتین ابھی بھی کم تر سمجھی جاتی ہیں۔ یہ عام سی بات ہے کہ جب عورت کی شادی ہو جائے تو ایمپلائیز اسے جاب چھوڑنے کا کہہ دیتے ہیں۔

During the 1960s and 1970s there was increasing pressure from women for equal rights.

1960 اور 1970 کے دوران عورتوں کی طرف سے برابری کے حقوق کا بہت دباؤ تھا۔

Parliament passed new laws giving women the right to equal pay and prohibiting employers from discriminating

پارلیمنٹ نے نئے قانون بنائے کہ عورت کو کم تر نہ سمجھا جائے اور برابر تنخواہ دی جائے

برطانیہ میں آج کی عورت
Women In Britain Today

Women in Britain today make up 51% of the population and 45% of the workforce.

برطانیہ میں خواتین کی آبادی 51% ہے۔ جبکہ کام کرنے والی عورتیں 45% ہیں۔

These days girls leave school, on average, with better qualifications than boys and there are now more women than men at university.

آج کل لڑکیاں لڑکوں کی نسبت تعلیم میں بہتر ہیں اور یونیورسٹی میں بھی لڑکیاں زیادہ ہیں۔

Although women continue to be employed in traditional female areas such as healthcare, teaching, secretarial and retail work.

البتہ عورتیں روایتی طور پر صحت، تعلیم، سیکریٹری اور ریٹیل کی فیلڈ میں کام کرتی ہیں۔

Research shows that very few people today believe that women in Britain should stay at home and not go out to work.

ریسرچ بتاتی ہے کہ بہت کم لوگ ہیں جو یہ کہتے ہیں کہ عورت کو گھر رہنا چاہیے اور کام نہیں کرنا چاہیے

Today, almost three-quarters of women with school-age children are in paid work.

آج تقریباً تین بٹا چار حصہ لڑکیاں سکول کی عمر میں کام کرتی ہیں۔

There is evidence that there is now greater equality in homes and that more men are taking some responsibility for raising the family and doing house work.

اس بات کا ثبوت ملا ہے کہ مرد بھی گھر سنبھالنے اور بچے پالنے کی ذمہ داری اٹھاتے ہیں۔

There are still examples of discrimination Women still do not always have the same access to promotion and better-paid jobs. The average hourly pay rate for women is 20% less than for men.

ابھی بھی کم تر سمجھے جانے کی مثالیں ملتی ہیں جیسا کہ خواتین کو پروموشن اور اچھی تنخواہ نہیں ملتی۔ ابھی بھی عورتوں کی تنخواہ مردوں سے 20% کم ہے۔

*51% are women and 49% are men *people can start paid work at the age of *14 pub may allow people to enter at the age of 14 but they can't drink

Chapter 2

بچے، فیملی اور نوجوان لوگ

Children, Family & Young People

In the UK, there are almost 15 million children and young people up to the age of 19. This is almost one quarter of the UK population.

یوکے میں تقریباً 15 ملین بچے ہیں جن کی عمر 19 سال سے کم ہے۔ جو کہ یوکے کی آبادی کا ایک بڑا چار حصہ ہے۔

Today, 65% of children live with both birth parents, almost 25% live in lone-parent families, and 10% live within a stepfamily.

اس وقت 65% بچے دونوں والدین کے ساتھ رہتے ہیں 25% ایک (والد یا والدہ) کے ساتھ رہتے ہیں 10% سوتیلی فیملی کے ساتھ رہتے ہیں۔

Most children in Britain receive weekly pocket money from their parent and many get extra money for doing jobs around the house.

بہت سے بچے اپنے والدین سے ہر ہفتے پاکٹ منی لیتے ہیں اور کچھ گھر کے کام وغیرہ کر کے فالتو پیسے کماتے ہیں۔

Children in the UK do not play outside the home as much as they did in the past. Part of the reason for this is increased home entertainment such as television, videos and computers.

بچے باہر اتنا نہیں کھیلتے جتنا پہلے کھیلتے تھے اس کی وجہ گھر میں تفریح ملنا جیسے ٹی وی وڈیو اور کمپیوٹر ہے۔

There is also increased concern for children safety and there are many stories in newspapers about child molestation by strangers, but there is no evidence that this kind of danger is increasing.

ایک وجہ بچوں کی سیفٹی کی فکر بھی ہے کہ آئے دن خبریں چھپتی ہیں کہ بچے کے ساتھ کوئی زیادتی نہ ہو جائے۔ لیکن ایسی کوئی بات نہیں کہ خطرہ بڑھ گیا ہے۔

*1/3 One third 33% as a whole population have tried illegal drugs *Half of young adults i.e. 50% have used illegal dugs *45% workforce are women

Education   تعلیم

The law states that children between the ages of 5 and 16 must attend school.

قانونی طور پر 5 سے 16 تک کے بچے کا سکول جانا لازمی ہے

Children take national tests in English, Mathematics and Science when they are 7, 11 and 14 years old.

14, 11, 7 سال کی عمر میں بچے انگلش میتھ اور سائنس کا ٹیسٹ پاس کرتے ہیں۔

Most young people take the General Certificate of Secondary Education (GCSE), or, in Scotland, Scottish Qualifications Authority (SQA) Standard Grade examinations when they are 16.

بہت سے بچے سولہ سال کی عمر میں جی سی ایس ای کا امتحان پاس کرتے ہیں سکاٹ لینڈ میں SQA کہتے ہیں

At 17 and 18, many take vocational qualifications, General Certificates of Education Advanced level (AGCEs), AS level

17, 18 سال کی عمر میں ووکیشنل تعلیم یا اے لیول پاس کرتے ہیں۔

One in three young people now go on to higher education at college or university.

تین میں سے ایک بچہ اعلیٰ تعلیم یا یونیورسٹی میں جاتا ہے۔

Gap year is a year out of education often includes voluntary work and travel overseas. Some young people work to earn and save money to pay for their university fees and living expenses.

گیپ ایئر میں طلباء تعلیم کو چھوڑ کر رضاکارانہ کام کرتے ہیں اور باہر سیر کیلئے جاتے ہیں کچھ کام کرتے ہیں تاکہ یونیورسٹی کی فیس اور اخراجات نکال سکیں۔

Work   کام

It is thought there are 2 million children at work at any one time.

تقریباً دو ملین بچے کام کرتے ہیں

Chapter 2   A Changing Society

7

Chapter 2

The most common jobs are newspaper delivery and work in supermarkets and newsagents.

عام طور پہ نیوز پیپر دیتے ہیں یا سپر مارکٹ میں کام کرتے ہیں۔

Many parents believe that part-time work helps children to become more independent as well as providing them (and sometimes their families) with extra income.

بہت سے والدین کا یہ خیال ہے کہ پارٹ ٹائم کام بچوں کو خود مختار بناتا ہے اور ساتھ ساتھ والدین کو کچھ پیسے بھی مل جاتے ہیں

Children can take up paid work not before 14

14 سال سے کم عمر کے بچے کام نہیں کر سکتے۔

Health Hazards ہیلتھ کے بارے میں خطرات

Many parents worry that their children may misuse drugs and addictive substances.

بہت سے والدین کو فکر رہتی ہے کہ ان کے بچے کہیں نشہ تو نہیں کرتے۔

Smoking سگریٹ نوشی

Although cigarette smoking has fallen in the adult population, more young are smoking and more girls smoke than boys.

اگرچہ سگریٹ نوشی نوجوانوں میں کم ہو گئی ہے مگر نوجوان بچے سگریٹ پیتے ہیں اور لڑکیاں لڑکوں کی نسبت زیادہ سگریٹ پیتی ہیں۔

By law, it is illegal to sell tobacco products to anyone under 16 years old.

قانونی طور پر سولہ سال سے کم عمر کو سگریٹ بیچنا جرم ہے۔

Alcohol شراب

Young people under the age of 18 are not allowed to buy alcohol.

18 سال سے کم عمر کے لوگ الکوحل نہیں خرید سکتے۔

*People can buy tobacco products at the age of 16 *People can have wine or bear with a meal in a hotel or restaurant at the age of 16 *People pass their GCSE at the age of 16

The amount of alcohol they drink at one time, known as binge drinking.

ایک ہی وقت میں اتنی شراب پینا کہ دھت ہو جائے بنج ڈرنکنگ کہلاتی ہے۔

It is illegal to be drunk in public and there are now more penalties to help control this problem, including on -the - spot fines.

پبلک پلیس پر پینا جرم ہے اس جرم کو کم کرنے کیلیے سزائیں اور موقع پر جرمانے کئے جاتے ہیں۔

illegal Drugs ڈرگ

Current statistics show that half of all young adults, and about a third of the population as a whole, have used illegal drugs at one time or another.

موجودہ اعدادو شمار کے مطابق آدھی تعداد میں جوان بچے نشہ کرتے ہیں جبکہ تین گنا یو کے لوگ ایک آدھ مرتبہ ڈرگ لے چکے ہیں۔

There is a strong link between the use of hard drugs (e.g. crack cocaine and heroin) and crime, and also hard drug and mental illness.

نشہ کرنے اور پھر جرم کرنا بہت ممکن ہے اور اس وجہ سے کوئی پاگل بھی ہو سکتا ہے۔

Young People's Political & Social Attitudes

جوان لوگوں کا پولیٹیکل اور سوشل رویہ

Young people in Britain can vote in elections from the age of 18.

اٹھارہ سال کی عمر میں ووٹ ڈالا جا سکتا ہے۔

In the 2001 general election, however only 1 in 5 first - time voters used their vote.

2001 میں پانچ میں سے ایک نے ووٹ کا استعمال کیا۔

Although most young people show little interest in party politics.

اگرچہ بہت سے جوان لوگ سیاست میں بہت کم دلچسپی رکھتے ہیں۔

Chapter 2

There is strong evidence that many are interested in specific political issues such as the environment and cruelty to animals.

اس بات کا ثبوت ملا ہے کہ کہ نوجوان لوگ خاص سیاسی مسائل جیسے کہ ماحولیات اور جانوروں کے ساتھ زیادتی پر فکر مند ہیں۔

In 2003 survey the five most important issues in Britain were crime, drugs, war/ terrorism, racism and health.

2003 کے سروے کے مطابق برطانیہ کو پانچ اہم مسائل کا سامنا ہے جیسا کہ جرم، منشیات، دہشت گردی نسلی فساد اور صحت۔

They found that 86% of young people had taken part in some form of community event over the past year, and 50% had taken part in fund-raising or collecting money for charity.

تقریباً 86% نوجوان لوگ کمیونٹی کے کاموں میں حصہ لیتے ہیں اور 50% چندہ اکٹھا کرنا اور چیریٹی کا کام کرنے میں حصہ لیتے ہیں۔

*People can vote at elections at the age of 18 *People can drink alcohol at the age of 18
*People can stand for the Office at the age of 18

(1) Why did the British Government encourage immigration in the late 1940s?
A. to help with the reconstruction after the World War II
B. because of the rebuilding Britain
C. to give refuge to people from communist countries
D. none of the above - the British Government did not encourage immigration

(2) Since when did women receive voting right at the same age as men?
A. 1882
B. 1928
C. 1918
D. 1948

(3) When did the Anglican Church come into existence?
A. In the 1720s
B. In the 1290s
C. In the 1530s
D. In the 1690s

(4) What date in November commemorates an event from 1605?
A. Remembrance Day, November 11
B. Mothering Sunday
C. Victory Day, November 20
D. Guy Fawkes Night, November 5

(5) In the 16th and 17th centuries, who came to Britain from France to escape political persecution?
A. Hungry labourers
B. Jews escaping pogroms
C. French Royal Family
D. Protestant Huguenots

(6) Since when are women allowed to vote?
A. 1882
B. 1928
C. 1918
D. 1948

(7) Where did most immigrants come from in the 1950s?
A. France, Italy and Spain
B. West Indies, India, Pakistan, Bangladesh
C. Russia and Scandinavia
D. United States, Canada, Australia, South Africa

(8) Between 1880 and 1910, who came to Britain from what are now Poland, Ukraine, and Belarus?
A. Jewish people escaping violence
B. Royalists
C. People of Indian origin to had been forced to leave
D. Liberal democrats

(9) When did the Queen's father die?
A. 1952
B. 1951
C. 1961
D. 1971

(10) A married woman had no right to divorce her husband until
A. 1957
B. 1857
C. 1956
D. 1958

(11) There has been an Assembly in Wales and a Parliament in Scotland since
A. 1790
B. the beginning of the 19th century
C. 1999
D. 1945

(12) What is the population of the United Kingdom (2005)?
A. just above 46 million people
B. around 70 million people
C. just under 34 million people
D. just under 60 million people

Chapter 2

(13) Women in Britain make up
A. 35% of the workforce
B. 51% of the workforce
C. 50% of the workforce
D. 45% of the workforce

(14) The average hourly pay for women is about
A. 10% lower than it is for men
B. 30% lower than it is for men
C. 20% lower than it is for men
D. The same as it is for men

(15) People under 19 represent
A. almost a third of the UK population
B. almost a quarter of the UK population
C. about 10% of the UK population
D. almost half of the UK population

(16) Is child molestation by strangers an increasing danger?
A. no, there is no evidence to support that claim
B. yes, because children play more often outside
C. only in Northern Ireland
D. yes, there is a strong increasing pattern

(17) How many children live with a single parent?
A. 25% of all children
B. 15% of all children
C. 35% of all chidren
D. 45% of all children

(18) Tobacco should not be sold to anyone under the age of
A. 14
B. 16
C. 18
D. 21

(19) What is mugging?
A. sitting in the street with a mug and begging for money
B. stealing from children
C. stealing in the street by threat or violence
D. any drug-related crime

(20) What is the largest in population part of the UK after England?
A. Wales
B. Northern Ireland
C. Midlands
D. Scotland

(21) Census records are confidential and anonymous, and can be consulted freely only after
A. 10 years
B. 50 years
C. Never
D. 100 years

(22) What percentage of the UK population is white?
A. 68%
B. 74%
C. 92%
D. 85%

(23) In London area, ethnic minorities comprise
A. 19% of all residents
B. 29% of all residents
C. almost 40% of all residents
D. 4.75% of all residents

(24) The Church of England is called, in Scotland and in the USA
A. Episcopal Church
B. Presbyterian Church
C. Anglican Church
D. Baptist Church

(25) In which area is Gaelic spoken?
A. in Highlands and Islands of Scotland
B. in Wales
C. in Greater London
D. nowhere, it's a dead language

(26) What is the name of the major tennis championship in the UK?
A. Roland Garros
B. Wimbledon Tennis Championship
C. Cup Final
D. Grand National Tennis Championship

(27) What is the name and the date of the National Day of Wales?
A. St George's Day, 23 April
B. St Andrew's Day, 30 November
C. St David's Day, 1 March
D. St Francis' Day, 19 June

(28) Who is the Supreme Governor of the Church of England?
A. The Prince of Wales
B. The Prime Minister
C. The Archbishop of Canterbury
D. The Queen

(29) What is the largest ethnical minority in Britain?
A. people of Caribbean descent
B. people of Pakistani descent
C. people of American descent
D. people of Indian descent

(30) What is celebrated on February 14th?
A. St Patrick's Day
B. February's Fool Day
C. St Valentine's Day
D. Remembrance Day

(31) When will the next census take place?
A. 2007
B. 2011
C. 2008
D. 2012

(32) Alcohol should not be sold to anyone under the age of
A. 18   B. 14   C. 16   D. 21

(33) What are the allowed religions in Britain?
A. Everyone has right to to practise the religion of their choice
C. Only Christianity
B. Christianity, Islam and Buddhism
D. Christianity and Islam

(34) What sports have a large following in the UK?
A. Hockey, chess, swimming
B. Football, rugby, cricket
C. Judo, badminton, volleyball
D. Basketball, tennis, rugby

(35) which of these statements are true?
A. In the 1950's centre were setup in the west Indies to recruit bus drivers
B. In the 1950,s centre were setup in India and Pakistan to recruit bus drivers

(36) When was the Second World War?
A 1840-1846   B 1901-1918   C 1919-1925   D 1939-1945

(37) Which of these statements is correct?
A Some young people work to pay for their university fees and expenses
B University education is free to anyone who studies

(38) When did married women gain the right to retain ownership of their own money and property?
A 1752
B 1792
C 1810
D 1882

(39) From which two locations did Britain admit refugees during the late 1960s?
A Ethiopia
B South East Asia
C Turkey
D Uganda

Chapter 2

(40) What percentage of the UK's population live in England%
 A 59% B 45%
 C 29% D 70%

(41) On average, boys leave school with better qualifications than girls. is this statement true or false?
 A True : B False

(42) Why did Irish migrants come to Britain during the mid 1840s?
 A To escape famine B To escape religious persecution
 C To invade and seize land" D to find job and shelter

(43) Who were Suffragettes?
 A Nurses that cared for the elderly B Representatives of people seeking asylum
 C Refugee care workers D Campaigners for greater rights for women

(44) What year did women in the UK gain the lo divorce their husband?
 A 1810 B 1857
 C 1901 D 1945

(45) Existing laws, women still do not always have the same access to promotion and better paid jobs as men.!o this statement true or false?
 A True B False

(46) What is the minimum age for buying tobacco?
 A 14 years old B 16 years old
 C 18 years old D 21 years old

(47) Why did Protestant Huguenots from France come to Britain?
 A To escape famine B To escape religious persecution
 C To invade and seize land D To seek refuge from war

(48) what percentage of children live in lone-parent families?
 A 10% B 25% C 40% D 55%

(49) Name three countries that Jewish people migrated from (and the UK) to escape persecution during 1880-1910
 A China, Japan, Korea B Israel, Egypt, Jordan
 C Poland, Ukraine, Belarus D USA, Canada, Mexico

(50) what proportion of young people enrol to go onto higher education after school?
 A One in two B One in three
 C One in four D All young people move on to higher education

1	2	3	4	5	6	7	8	9	10	11	12	13	14	15	16	17
A	B	C	D	D	C	B	A	A	B	C	D	D	C	B	A	A

18	19	20	21	22	23	24	25	26	27	28	29	30	31	32	33	34
B	C	D	D	C	B	A	A	B	C	D	D	C	B	A	A	B

35	36	37	38	39	40	41	42	43	44	45	46	47	48	49	50
A	D	A	D	B	D	B	B	D	B	A	C	B	B	C	B

Population آبادی

In 2005 the population of the United Kingdom was just under 60 million.

2005 میں یوکے کی آبادی 60 ملین سے کم تھی۔

The population has grown by 7.7% since 1971 and growth has been faster in more recent year

1971 سے آبادی 7.7% بڑھی ہے اور موجودہ سالوں میں اور اضافہ ہوا ہے۔

The general population in the UK has increased in the last 20 years, Although in some areas such as the North- East and North-West of England there has been decline

اگرچہ 20 سالوں میں آبادی بڑھی ہے مگر نارتھ ایسٹ اور نارتھ ویسٹ میں کمی ہوئی ہے

Both the birth rate and the death rate are falling and as a result the UK now has an ageing population. For instance, there are more people over 60 than children under 16. There is also a record number of people aged 85 and over

پیدائش اور اموات کی کمی ہوئی ہے اور جسکی وجہ سے یوکے میں بہت بوڑھے لوگ ہیں جیسے کہ 60 سال کی عمر کے لوگ 16 سال سے زیادہ ہیں۔ 85 سال سے زیادہ عمر کی تعداد بھی بہت ہے

The census مردم شماری

A census is a count of the whole population. It also collects statistics on topics such as age, place of birth, occupation, ethnicity, housing, health and marital status

سینسس تمام افراد کی گنتی ہے۔ اس میں عمر، برتھ پلیس، شعبہ، گھر، صحت اور شادی اسٹیٹس جیسی باتیں شامل ہوتی ہیں۔

A census has been taken every ten years since 1801, except during

---
* Key Points to remember in chapter 3
*Hogmanay is a happy new year in Scotland celebrated, 31 December and 2nd Jan is holiday
*Hanukkah is a Jewish festival *Chequers is the country house for Prime minister.

Chapter 3 UK-Today A Profile

15

CHAPTER 3

the Second World War. The next census will take place in 2011

سینسس ہر دس سال بعد ہوتا ہے سوائے ورلڈ وار ٹو کی جنگ کے۔ پہلا سینسس 1801 میں ہوا اور اگلا 2011 میں ہوگا

During a census, a form is delivered to every household in the country. This form asks for detailed information about each member of the household completed by law. The information remains confidential and must be anonymous it can be released to the public after 100 years

سینسس کے دوران ہر گھر کو ایک فارم بھیجا جاتا ہے۔ اس فارم میں گھر کے ہر فرد کے بارے میں معلومات دینی ہوتی ہیں جو کہ قانونی طور پر ضروری ہوتا ہے۔ یہ معلومات راز میں رہتی ہیں اور صرف سو سال بعد ہی بتائی جا سکتی ہیں۔

اقلیتی کثرت Ethnic diversity

People of Indian, Pakistani, Chinese, Black Caribbean, Black African, Bangladeshi and mixed ethnic descent make up 8.3% of the UK population. Today about half the members of these communities were born in the United Kingdom

ہندوستانی، پاکستانی، چینی، بلیک کیریبین، بلیک افریقن، بنگلہ دیشی اور مکس ملا کے اقلیتی آبادی یو کے کا 8.3% ہے۔ اس آبادی کا آدھا حصہ یو کے میں پیدا ہوتے ہیں۔

Large numbers have also arrived since 2004 from the new East European member states of the European Union

2004 میں نیوایسٹ یورپین ممبر اسٹیٹ یورپی یونین سے بڑی تعداد میں لوگ یو کے آئے۔

The figures from the 2001 census show that most members of the large ethnic minority groups in the UK live in England, where they make up 9% of the total population.

2001 کی مردم شماری سے پتہ چلتا ہے کہ زیادہ تر اقلیتی گروپس انگلینڈ میں رہتے ہیں جو کہ کل آبادی کا 9% ہے۔

*Scotland (8% of the population) 5.1 million .Wales (5% of the population) 2.9 million N. Ireland (3% of the population) 1.7 million. Total UK 59.8 million

45% of all ethnic minority people live in the London area, where they form nearly one - third of the population (29%).

اقلیتی آبادی لندن میں رہتی ہے جو کہ کل آبادی کا 29% ہے۔

Other areas of England with large ethnic minority populations are the West Midlands, the South East, the North West, and Yorkshire and Humberside.

انگلینڈ کے دوسرے اقلیتی آبادی والے علاقے میں ویسٹ مڈلینڈ، ساؤتھ ایسٹ، نارتھ ویسٹ، یوکشائر اور ہمبر سائڈ ہیں۔

Proportion of ethnic minority groups in the countries of the UK England 9% Wales 2% Scotland 2% Northern Ireland less than 1%

اقلیتی گروپس کا تناسب یوکے میں یہ ہے: انگلینڈ 9% ویلز 2% سکاٹ لینڈ 2% نارتھرن آئرلینڈ 1%

UK Nation and Origins یوکے کی قوم اور شہر

The longest distance on the mainland, from John O'Groats on the north coast of Scotland to Lands End in the south-west corner of England is about 870 Miles (approximately 1400 Kilometers)

جون اوگراٹ سے لیکر ساؤتھ ویسٹ انگلینڈ کے دوسرے کونے تک کا فاصلہ 870 میل ہے تقریباً 1400 کلومیٹر

Dialects in England are Geordie (Tyneside), Scouse (Liverpool) and Cockney (London). Many other languages in addition to English are spoken in the uk

Chapter 3 UK-Today A Profile

17

Chapter 3

انگلینڈ کے طرزِ کلام یہ ہیں جارڈی (ٹائن سائیڈ)، سکاؤس (لورپول)، کاکنی (لندن) اس کے علاوہ اور بھی زبانیں بولی جاتی ہیں۔

In Wales, too, an increasing number of people speak Welsh, which is taught in schools and universities.

ویلز میں ویلش بولی جاتی ہے جو کہ سکولوں اور یونیورسٹیوں میں پڑھائی جاتی ہے۔

In Scotland Gaelic is spoken in some parts of the Highlands and Islands and in Northern Ireland a few people speak Irish Gaelic

سکاٹ لینڈ میں آئی لینڈ میں گارلک بولی جاتی ہے کچھ لوگ آئریش گالک بولتے ہیں

Some of the dialects of English spoken in Scotland show the influence of the old Scottish language, Scots. One of the dialects spoken in Northern Ireland is Called Ulster Scots.

سکاٹ لینڈ کا پرانا لہجہ سکاٹس بھی ہے۔ ایک اور لہجہ جو سکاٹ لینڈ میں بولا جاتا ہے وہ ہے السٹر سکاٹ۔

Religion مذہب

In the 2001 census, just over 75% said they had a religion: 7 out of 10 of these were Christians 10% of the population attend religious services.

2001 کے سینسس میں 75% لوگوں نے کہا تھا کہ ان کا کوئی مذہب ہے جن میں 10 میں 7 لوگ کرسچن تھے۔ 10% لوگ مذہبی ہیں۔

More people attend services in Scotland and Northern Ireland than in England and Wales. In London the number of people who attend religious services is increasing.

انگلینڈ اور ویلز کی نسبت سکاٹ لینڈ اور نارتھرن آئرلینڈ میں لوگ زیادہ مزہبی ہیں۔ لندن میں جو لوگ ہیں وہ زیادہ مذہبی رسومات کی طرف بڑھ رہے ہیں۔

18

The official church of the state is the Church of England. The Church of England is called the Anglican Church. Episcopal Church in Scotland and in the USA. The Church of England is a Protestant church and has existed since the reformation in the 1530s.

ریاست کا سرکاری چرچ۔ چرچ آف انگلینڈ ہے۔ جس کو اینگلیکن چرچ بھی کہتے ہیں۔ سکاٹ لینڈ کا سرکاری چرچ اپی سکوپل چرچ ہے۔ انگلینڈ کا چرچ پروٹسٹنٹ چرچ ہے اور 1530 میں بنا تھا۔

The king or queen (the monarch) is the head, or Supreme Governor, of the Church of England. The monarch is not allowed to marry anyone who is not Protestant.

کنگ یا کوئین کو مونارک کہتے ہیں جو کہ چرچ آف انگلینڈ کا ہیڈ یا سپریم گورنر ہوتا ہے۔ مونارک کسی غیر پروٹسٹنٹ سے شادی نہیں کر سکتا۔

The spiritual leader of the Church of England is the Archbishop of Canterbury. The monarch has the right to select the Archbishop and other senior church officials, but usually the choice is made by the Prime Minister and a committee appointed by the Church

چرچ آف انگلینڈ کے روحانی پیشوا کو آرک بشپ آف کینٹابری کہتے ہیں۔

Several Church of England bishops sit in the House of Lords. In Scotland, the established church is the Presbyterian Church; its head is the Chief Moderator. There is no established church in Wales or in Northern Ireland.

انگلینڈ کے کئی بشپس ہاؤس آف لارڈ میں بیٹھتے ہیں۔ سکاٹ لینڈ میں چرچ کو پریسبائٹیرین چرچ کہتے ہیں اور چرچ کے ہیڈ کو چیف ماڈریٹر کہتے ہیں۔ ویلز اور ناردرن آئرلینڈ کا کوئی سرکاری چرچ نہیں ہے۔

Other Protestant Christian groups in the UK are Baptists, Presbyterians, Methodists and Quakers. 10% of Christians are Roman Catholic (40% in Northern Ireland).

Chapter 3

پروٹسٹنٹ کے اور فرقے : بپٹسٹ ، پریسبائٹیرین ، میتھاڈسٹ اور کوئکرز ہیں 10% رومن کیتھولک ہیں 40% نارتھرن آئرلینڈ میں ہیں ۔

Patron Saints   روحانی بزرگ

England, Scotland, Wales and Northern Ireland each have a national saint called a patron saint. These are not public holidays except for 17 March in Northern Ireland.

سب ملکوں کا قومی روحانی بزرگ ہے جن کو پیٹرن سینٹ کہتے ہیں اس دن چھٹی نہیں ہوتی سوائے 17 مارچ کے ۔

Patron saints' days

St David's day, Wales 1 March

St Patrick's day, Northern Ireland 17 March

St George's day, England 23 April

St Andrew's day, Scotland 30 November

There are also four public holidays a year called Bank Holidays

سال میں چار چھٹیاں ہوتی ہیں جن کو بینک ہولی ڈیز کہتے ہیں

Festivals and Traditions   میلے اور تہوار

The Notting Hill Carnival in west London and the Edinburgh Festival. Customs and traditions from various religions, such as Eid ul-Fitr (Muslim), Diwali (Hindu) and Hanukkah (Jewish) are widely recognised in the UK. Children learn about these at school. The main Christian festivals are Christmas and Easter

ناٹنگ ہل کارنیوال ، ایڈنبرگ فیسٹول ، یو کے کے فیسٹول ہیں اسی طرح عید مسلم مناتے ہیں ، دیوالی ہندو مناتے

20

ہیں، ہنوکا جیوز مناتے ہیں۔ بچے یہ سب سکول میں سیکھتے ہیں۔ انگلینڈ کے دو بڑے فیسٹول کرسمس اور ایسٹر ہیں

25 December, celebrates the birth of Jesus Christ. It is a public holiday. Many Christians go to church on Christmas Eve (24 December) or on Christmas Day itself. Christmas is also usually celebrated by people who are not Christian

25 دسمبر جیسس کی برتھ ڈے ہے۔ کرسچن چرچ جاتے ہیں 24 دسمبر کرسمس ایو ہے۔ جو لوگ کرسچن نہیں ہیں وہ بھی کرسمس مناتے ہیں۔

People usually spend the day at home and eat a special meal, which often includes turkey. They give each other gifts, send each other cards and decorate their houses. Many people decorate a tree. Christmas is a special time for children.

عام طور پہ لوگ گھر میں وقت گزارتے ہیں اور سپیشل میل ٹرکی کھاتے ہیں اور بہت سے لوگ ایک دوسرے کو گفٹ اور کارڈ دیتے ہیں اور درخت سجاتے ہیں۔

**Very young children believe that an old man, Father Christmas (or Santa Claus),
brings them presents during the night. He is always shown in pictures with a long white beard, dressed in red. Boxing Day, 26 December is the day after Christmas. It is a public holiday.**

چھوٹے بچے یہ سمجھتے ہیں کہ ایک اولڈ مین فادر کرسمس (سانٹا کلاس) ان کیلئے رات کو گفٹس لاتا ہے۔ جس کی لمبی سفید داڑھی ہوتی ہے اور سرخ لباس میں ہوتا ہے۔ 26 دسمبر کو باکسنگ ڈے کہتے ہیں اور اس دن چھٹی ہوتی ہے۔

New Year   نیا سال

1 January, is a public holiday. People usually celebrate on the night of 31 December. In Scotland, 31 December is called Hogmanay and 2 January is also a public holiday. In Scotland Hogmanay is a bigger Holiday For Some People Than Chirstmas

Chapter 3

نیو ایئر کم جنوری کو چھٹی ہوتی ہے۔ لوگ 31 دسمبر کی رات کو مناتے ہیں سکاٹ لینڈ میں 31 دسمبر کو ہوگنے کہتے ہیں اور دو جنوری کو بھی چھٹی ہوتی ہے۔ کچھ لوگ اسے کرس مس سے بڑا موقع مانتے ہیں۔

Valentine's Day

14 February, is when lovers exchange cards and gifts. Sometimes people send anonymous cards to some one they secretly admire.

ویلنٹائین ڈے 14 فروری کو مناتے ہیں جب محبت کرنے والے ایک دوسرے کو کارڈز دیتے ہیں کبھی کبھی اپنا نام راز میں رکھ کر جس کو پسند کرتے ہیں اسے کارڈ بھیجتے ہیں۔

April Fools Day اپریل فول ڈے

1 April, is a day when people play jokes on each other until midday. Often TV and newspapers carry stories intended to deceive credulous viewers and readers.

کم اپریل کو فول ڈے منایا جاتا ہے جب لوگ ایک دوسرے کو مڈ ڈے تک بیوقوف بناتے ہیں ٹی وی اور نیوز والے بھی مذاق کرتے ہیں

Mother's Day مدر ڈے

The Sunday three weeks before Easter is a day when children send cards or buy gifts for their mothers. Easter is also an important Christian festival.

مدرز ڈے تھری ویکس پہلے سنڈے کو منایا جاتا ہے۔ بچے ماں کو کارڈ دیتے ہیں۔ ایسٹر بھی ایک اہم کرسچن فیسٹول ہے۔

Hallowe'en ہیلوویین

31 October, is a very ancient festival. Young people will often dress up in frightening costumes to play 'trick or treat'. Giving them sweets or chocolates might stop them playing a trick on you. Sometimes people carry lanterns made out of pumpkins with a candle inside.

ہیلوین 31 اکتوبر کو منائی جاتی ہے۔ بچے ٹرک اینڈ ٹریٹ کھیلتے ہیں اور ڈراتے ہیں۔ ان کو سویٹس دینے سے وہ آپ کو ڈرانا بند کر دیتے ہیں۔ کبھی کبھی پمپکن میں لالٹین بنا کر پھرتے ہیں۔

Guy Fawkes Night گائے فوکس نائیٹ

5 November, is an occasion when people in Great Britain set off fireworks at home or in special displays. The origin of this celebration was an event in 1605, when a group of Catholics led by Guy Fawkes failed in their plan to kill the Protestant king with a bomb in the Houses of Parliament.

5 نومبر کو لوگ فائر ورک کرتے ہیں یہ ایک واقع کی یاد میں کرتے ہیں جب ایک کیتھولک گائے فاکس نے پارلیمنٹ میں پروٹسٹنٹ کنگ کو بم سے مارنے کا ناکام پلان بنایا تھا۔

Remembrance Day ریمیمبرینس ڈے

11 November, commemorates those who died fighting in World War 1, World War 2 and other wars. Many people wear poppies (a red flower) in memory of those who died. At 11a.m. there is a two - minute silence.

11 نومبر جنگوں میں مرنے والوں کی یاد میں منایا جاتا ہے۔ بہت سے لوگ مرنے والوں کی یاد میں سرخ پھول اپنے کالر پر سجاتے ہیں اور 11 بجے 2 منٹ کی خاموشی اختیار کی جاتی ہے۔

There are no United Kingdom teams for football and rugby. England, Scotland, Wales and Northern Ireland have their own teams.

یو کے کی اپنی کوئی ٹیم نہیں انگلینڈ، سکاٹ لینڈ، آئیر لینڈ، اور ویلز کی اپنی ٹیمیں ہیں۔

Sporting Events سپورٹس

Important sporting events include, the Grand National horse race, the Football Association (FA) cup final (and equivalents in Northern Ireland, Scotland and Wales), the Open golf championship and the Wimbledon tennis tournament

کھیلوں کے اہم نام یہ ہیں گرینڈ نیشنل ہارس ریس، فٹبال کپ FA اوپن گولف چیمپین شپ اور ویمبلڈن ٹینس

UK population 2001 Million UK Population

	Million	%
White (People of European, Australian, American descent)	54.2	92
Mixed	0.7	1.2
Asian or Asian British		
Indian	1.1	1.8
Pakistani	0.7	1.3
Bangladeshi	0.3	0.5
Other Asian	0.2	0.4
Black or Black British		
Black Caribbean	0.6	1.0
Black African	0.5	0.8
Black other	0.1	0.2
Chinese	0.2	0.4
Other	0.2	0.4

Religions in the UK %

Christian (10% of whom are Roman Catholic)	71.6
Muslim	2.7
Hindu	1.0
Sikh	0.6
Jewish	0.5
Buddhist	0.3
Other	0.3
Total All	77
No religion	15.5
Not stated	7.3

1 What is the name of the patron saint of Scotland?
A St Andrew   B St David C St George D St Patrick

2 When is Mother's Day?
A The Saturday four weeks before Easter B The Sunday four weeks before Easter
C The Sunday one week before Easter D The Sunday three weeks before Easter

3 When are general elections held?
A At least every year B At least every four years
C At least every five years   D At least every ten years

4 When is Hallowe'en celebrated?
A 1 March   B 31 October
C 1 November   D 30 November

5 What is the title of the King or Queen within the Church of England?
A Archbishop of Canterbury   B Governor General
C Head Priest   D Supreme Governor

6 According to the 2001 Census, what percentage of the UK population are Christians?
A   About 50%   B   About 90%
C   About 70%   D   About 20%

7 When is Christmas celebrated?
A 1 January B 24 December C 25 December D 25 November

8w What is the name of the patron saint of Northern Ireland?
A St Andrew B St David C St George D St Patrick

9 What proportion of women with children (of ochool age) are in paid work?
A Half   B One quarter
C Three quarters   D Two thirds

10 Whore is the Scouse dialect spoken?
A Cornwall B Liverpool C London D Tyneside

11 When is Guy Fawkes Night?
A The evening of 15 October
B The evening of 25 September C The evening of 30 May D The evening of 5 November

12 What is the largest ethnic minority in Britain?
A Bangladeshi descent B Black Caribbean descent C Indian descent D Pakistani descent

13 What percentage of the UK's ethnic minorities live in the London arc.iV
A 14% B 30% C 45% D 60%

14 Traditionally happens on April Fool's Day?
A It is a public holiday until noon B People enjoy public fireworks displays
C People play jokes on each other D None of the above

15 Where is the Welsh language widely spoken?
A Highlands and Islands of Scotland   B Ireland
C Southern England   D Wales

16 Britain ha Which country of the UK has the highest proportion o' "Untie minority groups in its population?
A England   B Wales
C 'ScotlandD   Northern Ireland

17 Is an ageing population and has a record number of people aged 85 and over. Is this statement true or false?
A True B False

18 What is the population of England?
A 23.4 million B 38.1 million C 50.1 million D 58.8 million

19 Who is the current heir to the throne?
A Prince William B The Duke of Edinburgh C The Duke of York D The Prince of Wales

20 When is Valentine's Day?
A 1 April B 1 February C 14 April D 14 February

21 Whore is the Scouse dialect spoken?
A Cornwall B   Liverpool C   London D Tyneside
22 What sport is played at the Wimbledon tournament?
A   Cricket B   Football C   Rugby D Tennis
23 What percentage of Christians in the UK are Roman Catholic?
A 10% B 20% C 30% D 40%
24 Which Of these statement True
A Boxing day Day and New Year are both public holidays
B New Year is a public holiday and Boxing Day is not
25 Where is the Cockney dialect spoken?
A Cornwall B   Liverpool C   London D Tynesid
26 Why was a census not carried out in the United Kingdom in 1941?
A   Because Britain was at war B   Because it was abolished by the government
C   Because it was boycotted by the public D   25 No census was planned for that year
27 What is Grand National?
A tennis tournament   B Footballcup
C golf championship   D Horse race
28 WHAT DOES Remembrance Day commemorate?
A The   appreciations of single mothers   B celebration of community
C cruciflixion of Jesus Christ   D the memory of those who died fighting in wars
29   What percentage of the UK population is made up of ethnic minorities
A   About 15 %   B   About 2%   C   About 25%
D About 8%
30 What do people sometimes do on Valentine's Day?
A   Fast from eating for the whole day   B   Play jokes on each other until midday
C Send anonymous cards to someone they secretly admire
D Wear poppies in memory of St Valentine
31 How might you stop young people playing tricks on you at Hallowe'en?
A CALL THE police B Give them some money
C Give them sweets or chocolates   D Hide from them
32 What does the abbreviation FA stand for?
A Federal Agent   B The Fine Arts
C THE FOOTBALL ASSOCIATION   D The Fourth Amendment
33 What percentage of the UK population say they attend religious services?
A Around 10%   B Around 20%
C Around 30%   D Around 40%
34 What traditionally happens on Mother's Day?
A Mothers make special meals for their families
B People celebrate the mother of Jesus Christ
C People give cards or gifts to their mothers
D People hold fireworks displays

1 A	2 D	3 B	4 B	5 D	6 C	7 C	8 D	9 D
10 B	11 D	12 C	13 C	14 C	15 D	16 A	17 A	18 C
19 D	20 D	21 B	22 D	23 A	24 C	25 A	26 D	27 D
28 D	29 C	30 C	31 C	32 A	33 C			

How UK Governs   برطانیہ کا طرز حکومت

More recently, devolved administrations have been set up for Scotland Wales and Northern Ireland.

کچھ عرصہ پہلے ہی سکاٹ لینڈ، ویلز اور ناردرن آئرلینڈ کیلئے ڈیولوڈ گورنمنٹ سیٹ کی گئی ہے۔

The British Constitution is not written down in any single document

برٹش گورنمنٹ دستور کی پالیسی کسی جگہ نہیں لکھی ہوئی۔

The Monarcy   بادشاہت

Queen Elizabeth II is the Head of State of the United Kingdom. She is also the head of many Countries in the Commonwealth.

کوئین الزبتھ دوئم نہ صرف یو کے کی ہیڈ ہے بلکہ بہت سے کامن ویلتھ کے ممالک کی بھی ہیڈ ہے۔

The UK, like Denmark, the Netherlands, Norway, Spain and Sweden, has a constitutional monarchy. Constitutional monarchy means that the king or queen does not rule the country, but appoints the government which the people have in democratic chosen in democratic elections.

یو کے، ڈنمارک، نیدرلینڈ، ناروے، سپین اور سویڈن میں بادشاہی راج ہے۔ اس کا مطلب ہے کہ کنگ یا کوئن حکومت نہیں چلاتے بلکہ گورنمنٹ چنتے ہے جو ڈیموکریٹک الیکشن میں جیت کر آتی ہیں

The queen or king can advise, warn and encourage the Prime Minister, the decision on government policies are made by the Prime minitser and cabinet

کنگ یا کوئین صرف مشورہ دے سکتے ہیں خبردار اور حوصلہ افزائی کر سکتے ہیں۔ گورنمنٹ پالیسی کے اوپر فیصلے پرائم منسٹر اور کابینہ کرتی ہے۔

The Queen has reigned since her father's death in 1952. Prince Charles, her oldest son, is the heir to the throne.

ملکہ نے 1952 میں اپنے والد کی وفات کے بعد حکومت سنبھالی۔ پرنس چارلس (پرنس آف ویلز) ملکہ کا بڑا بیٹا مستقبل کا بادشاہ ہے۔

*There are 78 seats for representatives from the UK
*The Prime Minister appoints about 20 senior MPs to become ministers of cabinet.
*Chancellor of the Exchequer, responsible for the economy,

27

Chapter 4

The Queen has important ceremonial roles such as the opening of the new parliamentary session each year. On this occasion the Queen makes a speech that summarises the government's policies for the year ahead.

ملکہ کا کام ہر سال پارلیمنٹ میں افتتاحی تقریب کا فیتا کاٹنا اور اس موقع پر گورنمنٹ پالیسی کے اوپر تقریر کرنا ہے۔

Government گورنمنٹ

The UK is divided into 646 parliamentary constituencies and at least every five years voters in each constituency elect their Member of Parliament (MP) in a general election.

یوکے کے 646 پارلیمانی حلقے ہیں جن میں ہر پانچ سال کے بعد الیکشن میں عوام اپنا پرائم منسٹر چنتی ہیں۔

All of the elected MPs form the House of Commons. Most MPs belong to political party and the party with the largest number of MPs forms the government

تمام ایم پی بل کر ہاؤس آف ایم پی بناتے ہیں۔ زیادہ تر ایم پی کا تعلق سیاسی جماعت سے ہوتا ہے۔ سب سے زیادہ ووٹ لینے والی جماعت حکومت بناتی ہے۔

House Of Common ہاؤس آف کامن

The House of Commons is the more important of the two chambers in Parliament

ہاؤس آف کامن زیادہ اہم ہے ہاؤس آف لارڈ کی نسبت۔

MPs have a number of different responsibilities. They represent everyone in their constituency, they help to create new laws, they scrutinize and comment on what the government is doing, and they debate important national issues.

*UK is divided into 646 parliamentary constituencies
*Every 5 years voters elect their Member of Parliament (MP) in a general election
*European Parliament elections are also held every five years

ایم پی کے بہت کام ہیں یہ ہر ایک کی اپنے حلقے میں نمائندگی کرتے ہیں۔ یہ نئے قوانین بنانے میں مدد کرتے ہیں گورنمنٹ کی کارکردگی چیک کرتے ہیں اور اپنے خیالات کا اظہار کرتے ہیں۔

الیکشن Election

If an MP dies or resigns, there will be another election, called a by-election, in his or her constituency. MPs are elected through a system called 'first past the post'.

جب ایم پی مر جائے یا ریزائن کر دے تو اس حلقے میں بائی الیکشن کروائے جاتے ہیں۔ ایم پی فرسٹ پاس دا پوسٹ (پہلے ووٹ لو) سسٹم کے تحت الیکٹ ہوتے ہیں

دی وپس The Whips

The Whips are a small group of MPs appointed by their party leaders. They are responsible for discipline in their party and making sure MPs attend the House of Common to vote.

وپس ایم پی کا ایک سمال گروپ ہے جسکو پارٹی لیڈر چنتا ہے۔ ان کی ذمہ داری ڈسپلن قائم کرنا ہے اور اس بات کی یقین دہانی کرنا کہ ایم پی ووٹ دینے کیلئے ہاؤس آف کامن اٹینڈ کریں۔

The Chief Whip often attends Cabinet or Shadow Cabinet meetings and arranges the schedule of proceedings in the House of Commons with the Speaker

چیف وپ اکثر کابینہ یا شیڈو کابینہ کی میٹنگز اٹینڈ کرتا ہے اور ہاؤس آف کامن میں سپیکر کے ساتھ شیڈیول طے کرتا ہے۔

Elections for the European Parliament are also held every five years. There are 78 seats for representatives in the UK.

یورپین پارلیمنٹ کے الیکشن بھی پانچ سال کے بعد ہوتے ہیں اور یوکے کی یورپ میں 78 سیٹیں ہیں

The Lord Chancellor, who is the minister responsible for legal affairs, is also a member of the Cabinet ut sits in the House of Lords rather than the House of Commons *The electoral register is updated very year in September or October *Local elections are held every year on 15 October.

Chapter 4

The European Parliament elected members are called Members of the European Parliament (MEPs). Elections to the European Parliament use a system of proportional representation.

ممبر آف یورپین پارلیمنٹ کو ایم ای پی کہتے ہیں۔ یورپین الیکشن متناسب سسٹم کی نمائندگی کرتا ہے۔

The House Of Lords   ہاؤس آف لارڈز

Members of the House of Lords, known as peers, are not elected and do no represent a constituency. Until 1958 all peers were either hereditary, senior judges, or bishops of the Church of England.

ممبر آف ہاؤس آف لارڈ کو پیرز کہتے ہیں۔ 1958 تک پیرز وراثتی تھے جن میں بشپس اور سینئر جج تھے۔

Since 1958 the Prime Minister has had the power to appoint peers just for their own life time. These peers, had a distinguished career in politics, business, law or some other profession.

1958 سے پرائم منسٹر کے پاس اختیارات ہیں کہ وہ اپنے لئے لائف ٹائم پیر چنے۔ پیر کا شاندار کیریئر سیاست میں کاروبار، قانون یا کسی اور پروفیشنل میں ہوتا ہے۔

Life peers are appointed by the Queen on the advice of Prime Minister in the last house years the hereditary peers have lost the automatic right to attend the few common.

لائف پیر پرائم منسٹر کے مشورے سے پیرز خود چنتی ہے۔ کچھ سالوں سے پیرز خود بخود ہاؤس آف لارڈ میں جانے کا حق کھو چکے ہیں۔

While the House of Lords is usually the less important of the two chambers of Parliament, It can suggest amendments or propose new laws, which are then discussed by the House of Commons.

ہاؤس آف لارڈ کم اہم ہے پارلیمنٹ میں۔ یہ تجاویز اور پروپوزل پیش کر سکتا ہے جو کہ ہاؤس آف کامن ڈسکس کرتا ہے۔

The House of Lords can become very important if the majority of its members will not agree to pass a law for which the House of Commons has voted.

ہاؤس آف لارڈ بہت اہم ہو جاتا ہے جب زیادہ ترممبر راضی نہ ہوں اس بات پر جو ہاؤس آف کامن نے ووٹ کی ہو۔

*The Home Secretary, responsible for law, order and immigration,
*The Foreign Secretary, responsible for Foreign Affairs, Ministers (called 'Secretaries of State') for education, health and decence.

The House of Commons has powers to overrule the House of Lords, but these are very rarely used.

ہاؤس آف کامن کے پاس پاور ہے کہ وہ ہاؤس آف لارڈ کو اوور رول کر جائے۔ لیکن ایسا بہت کم ہوتا ہے۔

The Prime Minister   پرائم منسٹر

The Prime Minister (PM) is the leader of the political party in power. He or she appoints the members of the Cabinet and has control over many important public appointments.

پرائم منسٹر پارٹی کا لیڈر ہوتا ہے، کابینہ بناتا ہے اور کافی اداروں پر کنٹرول ہوتا ہے۔

The official home of the Prime Minister is 10 Downing Street, in central London, near the Houses of Parliament; he or she also has a country house not far from London called Chequers.

پرائم منسٹر کا سرکاری گھر 10 ڈاؤننگ سٹریٹ سینٹرل لندن میں ہے پارلیمنٹ ہاؤس کے سامنے۔ اس کا ایک کنٹری ہاؤس بھی ہوتا ہے لندن کے قریب جسے چیکرز کہتے ہیں۔

The Prime Minister resigns when his or her party is defeated in a general election.

پرائم منسٹر ریزائن کر دیتا ہے جب اس کی پارٹی الیکشن میں ہار جاتی ہے۔

The Cabinet   دی کیبنٹ

The Prime Minister appoints about 20 senior MPs to become ministers in charge of departments.

پرائم منسٹر 20 ایم پی چنتا ہے جو کہ مختلف اداروں کے انچارج بنتے ہیں۔

These include the Chancellor of the Exchequer, responsible for the economy, the Home Secretary, responsible for law, order and immigration, the Foreign Secretary, responsible for Foreign Affairs, and ministers (called 'Secretaries for education, health and defence State').

چانسلر آف ایکسچکر دولت کیلئے ذمہ دار ہے۔ ہوم سکریٹری قانون اور امیگریشن کا ذمہ دار ہے۔ فارن سیکرٹری ملک سے باہر معاملات کا ذمہ دار ہے۔ منسٹر (جن کو سیکرٹری آف دی سٹیٹ کہتے ہیں) جیسے تعلیم کیلئے صحت کیلئے اور دفاع کیلئے۔

*Most of the money for the local authority services comes from the government through taxes. Only about 20% is funded locally through 'council tax' *The government began programme of devolved administration(devolving power in 1997

Chapter 4 How UK Governs

31

Chapter 4

The Lord Chancellor, who is the minister responsible for legal affairs, is also a member of the Cabinet but sits in the House of Lords rather than the House of Commons

لارڈ چانسلر جو لیگل افیرکا ذمہ دار ہے کابینہ کا بھی ممبر ہے لیکن ہاؤس آف لارڈ میں بیٹھتا ہے۔

The Cabinet, a small committee which usually meets weekly and makes important decisions about government policy.

کابینہ ایک چھوٹی کمیٹی ہے۔ جسکی ہر ہفتے میٹنگ ہوتی ہے جس میں گورنمنٹ پالیسی کے فیصلے ہوتے ہیں۔

The Opposition — دی اپوزیشن

The second largest party in the House of Commons is called the Opposition.

دوسری بڑی پارٹی ہاؤس آف کامن میں اپوزیشن کی ہوتی ہے۔

The Leader of the Opposition leads his or her party in pointing out the government's failures and weaknesses.

اوپوزیشن پارٹی گورنمنٹ کی ناکامی اور کمزوری پر بات کرتی ہے۔

Prime Minister Questions which takes place every week while Parliament is sitting.

پرائم منسٹر سوال ہر ہفتے ہوتا ہے جب پارلیمنٹ بیٹھی ہوتی ہے۔

The Leader of the Opposition also appoints senior Opposition MPs to lead the criticism of government ministers, and together they form the Shadow Cabinet.

شیڈو کابینہ میں سینیئر ایم پی گورنمنٹ اور پرائم منسٹر پر نقطہ چینی کرتے ہیں۔

The Speaker — دی سپیکر

Debates in the House of Commons are chaired by the Speaker, who is the chief officer of the House of Commons. The Speaker is politically neutral.

سپیکر جو کہ چیف آفیسر ہوتا ہے بحث سنتا ہے اور وہ نیوٹرل ہوتا ہے۔

Speaker is an MP, elected by fellow MPs to keep order during political debates and to make sure the rules are followed.

سپیکر ایک ایم پی ہوتا ہے اور ساتھی ایم پی اسے چنتے ہیں اس کا کام آرڈر رکھنا اور یقین کرنا کہ سب کام نظام سے چل رہا ہے۔

*Commonwealth, which currently has 53 member
*Mandatory services are Education, Housing, Social services, Transport Fire service, rubbish collection.

This includes making sure the Opposition has a guaranteed amount of time to debate issues it chooses. The Speaker is politically neutral and he/she represents Parliament at ceremonial occasions.

اس کا کام ہے کہ اپوزیشن کو پورا وقت ملے۔ سپیکر پارلمنٹ میں تقریب کے موقع پر نمائندگی کرتا ہے۔ اور سیاسی طور پر نیوٹرل ہوتا ہے

The Party System   دی پارٹی سسٹم

Anyone can stand for election as an MP but they are unlikely to win an election unless they have been nominated to represent one of the major political party

کوئی بھی ایم پی کے الیکشن میں کھڑا ہوسکتا ہے لیکن جیتنا مشکل ہوتا ہے جب تک کہ کسی سیاسی پارٹی سے تعلق نہ ہو۔

These are the Labour Party, the Conservative Party, the Liberal Democrats, or one of the parties representing Scottish, Welsh, or Northern Irish interests.

لیبر پارٹی ۔ کنزرویٹو پارٹی ۔ لبرل ڈیموکریٹس ۔ پارٹی جو کہ سکاٹ، ویلش یا ناردرن آئرش کی نمائندگی کرتی ہے۔

There are just a few MPs who do not represent any of the main political parties and are called 'independents'.

جو کسی پارٹی کے ساتھ نہیں ہے وہ آزاد ہے

Pressure & Lobby Group

Pressure and lobby groups are organisations that try to influence government policy. They play a very important role in poltics

پریشر گروپ تنظیم گورنمنٹ پالیسی پر اثر انداز ہوتی ہیں۔ سیاست میں ان کا اہم رول ہے۔

The general public is more likely groups than join a political party to support pressure.

عام لوگ سیاسی پارٹی کی نسبت پریشر گروپ کو سپورٹ کرتے ہیں۔

The Civil Service   دی سول سروسز

Civil servants are managers and administrators who carry out government policy.

سول ملازم مینیجر ہوتے ہیں جو گورنمنٹ پالیسی پر عمل کرتے ہیں۔

*Euoropean parliament has got 78 seats for representatives from England * There are 129 members of Scottish Parliament and the Scottish assembly is in Edinburgh Scottish Parliament can pass legislation for Scotland on all matters that are not specifically reserved

Chapter 4

They have to be politically neutral and professional, regardless of which political party is in power.

سیاسی طور پہ یہ نیوٹرل ہوتے ہیں اور پروفشنل ہوتے ہیں چاہے جو بھی پارٹی ہو۔

Although civil servants have to follow the policies of the elected government, they warn ministers if they think a policy is impractical or not in the public interest.

اگر چہ گورنمنٹ پالیسی پہ عمل کرتے ہیں۔ یہ خبردار کر سکتے ہیں اگر کوئی پالیسی عوام کے خلاف ہو۔

Devolved Administration   چھوٹی سطح پر انتظامیہ

In 1997 the government began a programme of devolving power from central government.

1997 میں گورنمنٹ نے ڈیولوڈ سسٹم شروع کیا۔

Since 1999 there has been a Welsh Assembly, a Scottish Parliament and, periodically, a Northern Ireland Assembly.

1999 سے ویلش، سکاٹش اور بعد میں ناردرن آئرلینڈ اسمبلی وجود میں آئی۔

Although policy and laws governing defence, foreign affairs, taxation and social security all remain under central UK government control

اگر چہ پالیسی، قانون برائے دفاع، ملک سے باہر کے معاملات، ٹیکس اور سوشل سکیورٹی یوکے کے پاس ہیں۔

The Welsh Assembly Government

The National Assembly for Wales, or Welsh Assembly Government (WAG), is situated in Cardiff the capital city of Wales. It has 60 Assembly Members (AMs) and elections are held every four years.

ویلش اسمبلی کارڈف میں ویلز کے شہر میں ہے۔ اس کے ساتھ 60 ممبر ہیں الیکشن ہر چار سال بعد ہوتے ہیں۔

*Since 1999 there has been a Whelsh Assembly, Scottish Parliment & northern Ireland Assembly. the election system is proportional representation in Whelsh Assembly, Scottish Parliament & Northern Ireland Assembly Euoropean parliament also use the system of proportional representation

34

The Assembly has the power to make decisions on important matters such as education policy, the environment, health services, transport and local government, and to pass laws for Wales on these matters

اس کے پاس پاور ہے کہ یہ تعلیم کی پالیسی ماحول ، صحت، ٹرانسپورٹ، لوکل گورنمنٹ کے قانون پاس کراسکے۔

Scotland Parliament سکاٹ لینڈ پارلیمنٹ

In 1999 the Parliament of Scotland, which sits in Edinburgh, the capital city of Scotland. There are 129 Members of the Scottish Parliament (MSPs), elected by a form of proportional representation.

1999 میں سکاٹ لینڈ کی پارلیمنٹ بنی جو ایڈنبرگ میں بھیٹتی ہے اس کے 129 ممبر ہیں۔ جن کو ایم ایس پی کہتے ہیں۔

The Scottish Parliament can pass legislation for Scotland on all matters that are not specifically reserved to the UK Parliament. The matters on which the Scottish Parliament can legislate include civil and criminal law, health, education, planning and the raising of additional taxes.

سکاٹ لینڈ کی پارلیمنٹ تمام معاملات پر قانون سازی کرسکتی ہے سوائے ان کے جو یو کے کی پارلیمنٹ میں ریزرو ہیں۔

Northern Ireland Assembly ناردرن آئرلینڈ اسمبلی

Northern Ireland Parliament was established in 1922 when Ireland was divided, but it was abolished in 1972 shortly after the Troubles broke out in 1969. The Assembly has 108 elected members known as MLAs (Members of the Legislative Assembly

ناردرن آئرلینڈ 1922 میں بنی لیکن 1972 میں ختم ہوگئی جب 1969 میں حالات خراب ہوے۔ اس کے ممبر 108 ہیں جنہیں ایم ایل اے کہتے ہیں۔

*Northern Ireland Parliament established in 1922 and it abolished (suspended) in 1972 when trouble broke in 1969 *Northern Ireland parliament has got 108 members and currently i.e 2006 assembly is suspended

Chapter 4 How UK Governs

Chapter 4

Decision Making powers devolved to Northern Ireland include education, agriculture, the environment, health and social services.

تعلیم، ماحول، صحت اور ساجی سروس پر قانون بنا سکتے ہیں۔

The UK government kept the power to suspend the Northern Ireland Assembly if the political leaders no longer agreed to work together or if the Assembly was not working in the interests of the people of Northern Ireland.

یو کے گورنمنٹ کے پاس پاور ہے کہ ناردرن آئر یلینڈ کی اسمبلی سسپنڈ کر سکتا ہے اگر پولیٹیکل لیڈر مل کر کام نہ کریں یا اسمبلی لوگوں کی بہتری کیلئے کام نہ کرے۔

Local Government — لوکل گورنمنٹ

Towns, cities and rural areas in the UK are governed by democratically elected councils, often called local authorities. Most larger towns and cities will have a single local authority.

قصبے، شہر اور دیہاتی علاقے کا نظام کونسل چلاتی ہیں۔ جنہیں لوکل اتھارٹی بھی کہا جاتا ہے۔

Mayor who is the ceremonial leader of the council but in some towns a mayor is appointed to be the effective leader of the administration. London has 33 local authorities.

مئیر کونسل کی تقاریب کا لیڈر ہوتا ہے۔ کچھ علاقوں میں با اثر ناظم بھی ہوتا ہے۔

Mandatory services include education, housing, social services, passenger transport, the fire service, rubbish collection, planning, environmental health and libraries.

مینڈیٹری سروس میں تعلیم، سوشل سروس، ٹرانسپورٹ، فائر سروس، ربش اکھٹا کرنا، پلاننگ، ہیلتھ اور لائبریری شامل ہوتی ہیں۔

Most of the money for the local authority services comes from the government through taxes. Only about 20% is funded locally through 'council tax.

---

*The Wales Assembly can make decisions on important matters i.e. education health environment transport and local govt and to pass laws for Wales within a statuary framework i.e. UK Parliament 60 Assembly members of Wales Assembly and the assembly is in Cardiff.

36

زیادہ تر پیسہ لوکل اتھارٹی کے لیے ٹیکسوں سے آتا ہے۔ صرف پیں فی صد پیسہ کونسل ٹیکس سے آتا ہے۔

It applies to all domestic properties, including houses, bungalows, flats, maisonettes, mobile home houseboats, whether owned or rented.

کونسل ٹیکس تمام قسم کی جائداد پر لاگو ہوتا ہے جیسے گھر، بنگلہ، فلیٹ، ہاؤس بوٹ وغیرہ۔

Local elections for councillors are held in May every year. Many candidates stand for council election as members of a political party.

The Judiciary   ججز

Judges (who are together called 'the judiciary)   جج مل کر جوڈیشری بناتے ہی

If they find that a public body is not respecting a person's human rights, they may order that body to change its practices and to pay compensation. If the judges believe that an Act of Parliament is incompatible with the Human Rights Act, they cannot change it themselves but they can ask Parliament to consider doing so.

اگر انہیں پتہ چلے کہ کوئی ادارہ انسانی حقوق کی خلاف ورزی کر رہا ہے تو وہ انہیں کہیں گے کہ ایسا نہ کریں اور ہرجانہ دیں۔ اگر جج کو ایسا لگے کہ پارلیمنٹ کا ایکٹ ہیومین رائٹس کے خلاف ہے تو وہ اسے چینج تو نہیں کر سکتے البتہ پارلیمنٹ کو کہہ سکتے ہیں کہ وہ چینج کرے۔

Judges cannot, however, decide whether people are guilty or innocent of serious crimes. When someone is accused a serious crime, a jury will decide whether he or she is innocent or guilty

جج اس بات کا فیصلہ نہیں کر سکتے کہ سنگین جرائم کرنے والے لوگ قصوروار ہیں یا بے گناہ۔ جب کسی پر جرم عائد ہوتا ہے تو جیوری فیصلہ کرتی ہے۔

If guilty, the judge will decide on the penalty. For less important crimes, a magistrate will decide on guilt and on any penalty.

اگر قصوروار ہو تو جج سزا سناتا ہے۔ عام جرائم کا فیصلہ اور سزا مجسٹریٹ سناتا ہے۔

The Police   پولیس

The police service is organized locally, with one police service for each county or group of counties.

پولیس سروس لوکل سطح پر کام کرتی ہے ہر ایک علاقے کی ایک پولیس ہوتی ہے۔

*The council of European Union and Council of Ministers are same. Council of ministers is the governing and legislative body of EU *The Council of Ministers passes EU law on the recommendations of the European Commission and the European Parliament and makes important decisions how to the EU is run.

Chapter 4

The Police   پولیس

The largest force is the Metropolitan Police, which serves London and is based at New Scotland Yard. Northern Ireland as a whole is served by the Police Service for Northern Ireland (PSNI).

سب سے بڑی پولیس فورس میٹروپولیٹن پولیس ہے جو لندن میں نیو سکاٹ لینڈ یارڈ میں واقع ہے۔ نادرن آئر لینڈ میں ایک ہی پولیس سروس ہے پولیس سروس فار نادرن آئر یلینڈ۔

The police have 'operational independence', which means that the government cannot instruct them on what to do in any particular case.

پولیس کے پاس اختیارات ہوتے ہیں مطلب یہ کہ گورنمنٹ انہیں ہدایات نہیں دیتی کہ کیا کرنا ہے اور کیا نہیں کرنا۔

Police authorities made up of councilors and magistrates. The Independent Police Complaints Commission (or, in Northern Ireland Ombudsman) investigates serious complaints against the police.

پولیس اتھارٹی کونسلر اور مجسٹریٹ پر مشتمل ہوتی ہے۔ آزادانہ پولیس کمیشن سنگین شکایات کی تحقیق کرتا ہے۔ نادرن آئر لینڈ میں اسے اومبسمین کہتے ہیں۔

Non-departmental public bodies (quangos)
Non-departmental public bodies, also known as quangos, are independent organisations that carry out functions on behalf of the public

نان ڈیپارٹمنٹل پبلک باڈیز کو انگوس بھی کہتے ہیں یہ آزاد تنظیم ہوتی ہیں جو کہ پبلک کیلئے کام کرتی ہیں۔

The Role Of The Media   میڈیا کا رول

Proceedings in Parliament are broadcast on digital television and published in official reports such as Hansard,

پارلیمنٹ کی بحث جو کہ ٹی وی پر دکھائی جاتی ہے اور اخبارات میں چھپتی ہے اسے ہینسرڈ کہتے ہیں۔

The UK has a free press, meaning that what is written in newspapers is free from government control.

یو کے کی آزاد پریس ہے مطلب یہ کہ جو بھی اخبار میں چھپتا ہے گورنمنٹ کے کنٹرول سے آزاد ہے۔

*Northern Ireland assembly can be suspended if the political parties no longer agree to work together.
*Northern Ireland Assembly can't pass any bills or make any decisions but it can deal matters with Education, agriculture, environment health and social services *European Economic Community and European Union are same

By law, radio and television coverage of the political parties at election periods must be balanced and so equal time has to be given to rival viewpoints.

قانونی طور پر سیاسی پارٹی کو الیکشن کے وقت ریڈیو اور ٹی وی پر پورا پورا وقت ملنا چاہیے۔

Who Can Vote — ووٹ کون کر سکتا ہے

The United Kingdom has had a fully democratic system since 1928, when women were allowed to vote at 21, the same age as men. The present voting age of 18 was set in 1969,

1928 سے یوکے میں ڈیموکریسی ہے جب عورت کو 21 سال کی عمر میں مردوں کی طرح ووٹ دینے کا حق ملا۔ اس وقت ووٹنگ کی عمر 18 سال ہے جو کہ 1969 میں سیٹ ہوئی تھی۔

Citizens of the UK, the Commonwealth and the Irish Republic (if resident in the UK) can vote in all public elections. Citizens of EU states who are resident in the UK can vote in all elections except national parliamentary

برطانیہ، کامن ویلتھ اور آئرش ریپبلک کے شہری تمام الیکشن میں حصہ لے سکتے ہیں۔ یورپین جو کہ برطانیہ کے رہائشی ہیں تمام الیکشن میں حصہ لے سکتے ہیں سوائے نیشنل پارلیمنٹ الیکشن کے۔

In order to vote in a parliamentary, local or European election, you must have your name on the register of electors

پارلیمنٹری، لوکل یا یورپین الیکشن میں حصہ لینے کیلئے آپ کا نام رجسٹر میں ہونا چاہیے۔

The Electoral Register — الیکٹرول رجسٹر

The electoral register is updated every year in September or October. An electoral registration form is sent to every household and it has to be completed and returned, with the names of everyone who is resident in the household

الیکٹرول رجسٹر ہر سال ستمبر، اکتوبر میں اپ ڈیٹ ہوتا ہے۔

*European Parliament examines decisions made by the European Council and the European commission. It also has power to refuse agreement proposed by the commission *It checks the spending of EU funds as well *EU directives are about the procedures for making workers redundant

Chapter 4

By law, each local authority has to make its electoral register available for anyone to look at. Although this now has to be supervised.

قانونی طور پہ ہر لوکل اتھارٹی کو الیکٹرول رجسٹر دکھانا پڑتا ہے البتہ کسی کی سپرویژن میں ہوتا ہے۔

Standing For Office — الیکشن میں کھڑے ہونا

Citizens 18 or over can stand for public office. To become a local councillor, a candidate must have a local connection with the area through work, being on the electoral register, or through renting or owning land or property.

اٹھارہ سال کی عمر میں الیکشن میں حصہ لے سکتے ہیں۔ لوکل کونسلر بننے کیلئے امیدوار کو مقامی لوگوں سے جان پہچان ہونی چاہئے الیکٹرول رجسٹر میں نام ہونا چاہئے یا کرائے پر مکان دے کر یا الیکٹر ریکارڈ میں ہونا چاہیے۔

Contacting Elected Members — منتخب نمائندے سے رابطہ

You can contact MPs by letter or phone at their constituency office or their office in the House of Commons.

آپ ایم پی سے لیٹر لکھ کر یا فون کر کے رابطہ کر سکتے ہیں

Many Assembly Members, MSPs, MPs and MEPs hold regular local 'surgeries'. These are often advertised in the local paper and constituents can go and talk about issues in person.

بہت سے اسمبلی ممبر لوکل سرجری کرتے ہیں جن کے بارے میں نیوز پیپر میں آتا ہے۔ سرجری میں لوگ جا کر اپنے مسائل بیان کرتے ہیں۔

You can either write to your local MP in advance to ask for tickets or you can queue on the day at the public entrance. Entrance is free.

آپ اگر ہاؤس آف کامن جانا چاہتے ہیں تو لوکل ایم پی کو لیٹر لکھ کر ٹکٹ منگوا سکتے ہیں یا پھر قطار میں کھڑے رہ کر اندر جا سکتے ہیں داخلہ فری ہے۔

Sometimes there are long queues for the House of Commons and you may have to wait for at least one or two hours. It is usually easier to get into the House of Lords.

کبھی کبھی لمبی قطار ہوتی ہے اور گھنٹوں انتظار کرنا پڑتا ہے۔ ہاؤس آف لارڈ میں جانا آسان ہوتا ہے۔

In Northern Ireland, elected members, known as MLAs, meet in the Northern Ireland Assembly at Stormont, in Belfast.

نادرن آئرلینڈ میں ممبرز کو ایم ایل اے کہتے ہیں ان کی اسمبلی بیلفاسٹ میں سٹارمنٹ میں ہوتی ہے۔

*United Nations (UN), an international organisation which has 190 countries *European Commission is the civil service of the EU and it drafts proposals for new EU policies and laws and admin its funding programmes *European commission is based in Brussels in Belgium.

In Scotland, the elected members, called MSPs, meet in the Scottish Parliament at Holyrood in Edinburgh

سکاٹ لینڈ میں ممبرز کو ایم ایس پی کہتے ہیں ان کی اسمبلی ایڈنبرگ میں ہولی روڈ میں ہوتی ہے۔

In Wales, the elected members, known as AMs, meet in the Welsh Assembly in the Senedd in Cardiff Bay

ویلز میں ممبرز کو اے ایم کہتے ان کی اسمبلی کارڈاف میں سینڈ میں ہے۔

The Commonwealth

The Commonwealth is an association of countries, most of which were once part of the British Empire.

کامن ویلتھ وہ ممالک ہیں جو کہ برٹش ایمپائر کا حصہ تھے۔

The Queen is the head of the Commonwealth, which currently has 53 member states. Membership is voluntary and the ommonwealth has no power over its members although it can suspend membership

ملکہ کامن ویلتھ کے ممالک کی سربراہ ہے اس کے 53 ممالک ہیں ممبر شپ رضاکارانہ ہے اور کامن ویلتھ کی کوئی پاور نہیں البتہ ممبر شپ سسپنڈ کر سکتا ہے۔

The Commonwealth aims to promote democracy, good government and to eradicate poverty.

کامن ویلتھ کا مقصد جمہوریت کا فروغ اچھی گورنمنٹ اور غربت کا خاتمہ ہے۔

The European Union (EU)

The European Union (EU), originally called the European Economic Community (EEC), was set up by six Western European countries who signed the Treaty of Rome on 25 March 1957.

یورپین یونین کو دراصل یورپین اکنامک کمیونٹی کہتے ہیں جو کہ چھے ممالک نے 25 مارچ 1957 کو بنائی تھی

One of the main reasons for doing this was the belief that co-operation between states would reduce the likelihood of another war in Europe

اس کو بنانے کی اصل وجہ یہ تھی کہ یورپ میں ایک اور جنگ نہ ہو جائے۔

Originally the UK decided not to join this group and only became part of the European Union in 1973. In 2004 ten new member countries joined the EU with a further two in 2006 making a total of 27 member countries

یو کے نے فیصلہ کیا کہ ممبر نہ بنے اسی لئے 1973 میں ممبر بنا۔ 2004 میں دس اور ممالک اس کا حصہ بن گئے اور 2006 میں دو اور ممبر بنے کل ملا کے 27 ممبر ہو گئے۔

*UN was set up after the Second World War and aims to prevent war and promote international peace and security. *UK is one of the five permanent members *Agreements produced from UN are Universal declaration of human rights, the convention of elimination of all form of discrimination against women & UN convention on the rights of the child

Chapter 4

One of the main aims of the EU today is for member states to function as a single market

ای یو کا مقصد آج ایک سنگل مارکیٹ کی طرح کام کرنا ہے۔

British people choose to accept the euro in a referendum.

برٹش لوگ صرف ریفرینڈم کے ذریعے ہی یورو کرنسی قبول کر سکتے ہیں

Citizens of an EU member state have the right to travel to and work in any EU country if they have a valid passport or identity card.

EU ممبر سٹیٹ   Eu Member State

The Council of the European Union (usually called the Council of Ministers) is effectively the governing body of the EU. It is made up of government ministers from each country in the EU and, together with the European Parliament is the legislative body of the EU.

کونسل آف یورپین یونین جس کو کونسل آف منسٹر بھی کہتے ہیں یورپین یونین کی گورننگ باڈی ہے۔ جو کہ ہر ملک سے چنے جاتے ہیں۔ جبکہ یورپین پارلیمنٹ ای یو کی لجسلیٹو باڈی ہے۔ گورنمنٹ منسٹر پر مشتمل ہوتی ہے

The Council of Ministers passes EU law on the recommendations of the European Comission and the European Parliament and takes the most important decisions about how the EU is run

کونسل آف منسٹر یورپین کمیشن اور یورپین پارلیمنٹ کی سفارش پر ای یو کے لاء پاس کرتی ہے۔ اور بہت اہم فیصلے جیسے کہ ای یو کو کیسے چلایا جائے

The European Commission is based in Brussels, the capital city of Belgium. It is the civil service of the EU and drafts proposals for new EU policies and laws and administers its funding programmes

یورپین کمیشن برسلز میں ہے جو کہ بیلجیم کا شہر ہے۔ یہ ای یو کی سول سروس ہے جو کہ نئی ای یو کی پالیسی اور فنڈنگ پروگرام کا ڈرافٹ بناتی ہے۔

The European Parliament meets in Strasbourg, in north-eastern France, and in Brussels. Each country elects members, called Members of the European Parliament (MEPs), every five years.

یورپین پارلیمنٹ کی میٹنگ سٹراسبرگ، نارتھ فرانس اور برسلز میں ہوتی ہے۔ ان کے ممبر کو ایم ای پی کہتے ہیں الیکشن ہر پانچ سال بعد ہوتے ہیں۔

*EU regulations that limit the number of hours people can be made to work. Council of Europe has no power to make laws but draws conventions and charters on human rights, democracy, education, the environment, health and culture. UK was one of the founder member.

42

The European Parliament examines decisions made by the European Council and the European Commission, and it has the power to refuse agreement to European laws proposed by the commission and to check on the spending of EU

یورپین پارلیمنٹ یورپین کونسل اور یورپین کمیشن کے فیصلے کا معائنہ کرتی ہے۔اوراس کے پاس پاور ہے کہ یورپین لاؤکو کینسل کرسکتی ہے اور یورپین یونین کےاخراجات کا حساب رکھتی ہے۔

European laws, called directives, regulations are directives about the procedures for making workers redundant and regulations that limit the number of hours people can be made to work.

یورپین لاؤکو ڈائیریکٹو اور ریگولیشن کہتے ہیں ڈائیریکٹو ایسا سسٹم جس میں کام کرنے والے کم ہوجائیں اور ریگولیشن یعنی ورکنگ آور کم کر دیں۔

The Council of Europe

The Council of Europe was created in 1949 and the UK was one of the founder members. Most of the countries of Europe are members.

کونسل آف یورپ 1949 میں بنی تھی اور یوکے اس کا بانی ممبر تھا۔

It has no power to make laws but draws up conventions and charters which focus on human rights, democracy, education, the environment, health and culture. The most important of these is the European Convention on Human Rights

اس کی کوئی پاور نہیں کہ قانون بنائے البتہ ایسے منصوبے اور تجاویز پیش کرتا ہے جو کہ انسانی حقوق،جمہوریت،تعلیم،ماحول،صحت اور کلچر کی عکاسی کریں۔سب سے اہم ان میں انسانی حقوق کا خیال کرنا

The United Nations (UN)

The UK is a member of the United Nations (UN), an international organisation to which over 190 countries now belong.

یوکے اقوام متحدہ کا ممبر ہے یہ بین الاقوامی تنظیم ہے جس کے 190 ممبر ہیں۔

The UN was set up after the Second World War and aims to prevent war and promote international peace and security.

یو این دوسری جنگ کے بعد بنائی گئی جس کا مقصد جنگ کی روک تھام اور انٹرنیشنل امن اور تحفظ قائم کرنا ہے۔

*Bank notes in the UK come in denominations (values) of £5, £10, £20 and £50. UK will adopt the euro if British people vote for the euro in referendum *Social fund helps people with the cost of moving and setting up home.

43

Chapter 4

There are 15 members on the UN Security Council, which recommends action by the UN when there are international crises and threats to peace. The UK is one of the five permanent members

یو این سیکیورٹی کونسل کے 15 ممبر ہیں۔ جب امن کو خطرہ لاحق ہو یا انٹرنیشنل حالات خراب ہو جائیں تو یہ ایکشن لیتی ہے۔ یوکے کے پانچ ممبروں میں سے اس کا پرمانینٹ ممبر ہے۔

Three very important agreements produced by the UN are the Universal Declaration of Human Rights, the Convention on the Elimination of All Forms of Discrimination against Women, and the UN Convention on the Rights of the Child.

یو این کے تین بہت اہم معاہدے انسانی حقوق کا فروغ، خواتین کی ہر موقع پر برابری نہ ہونے کی حوصلہ شکنی اور بچوں کے حقوق کا قانون ہے۔

Answers for Practice Test.

1A	2B	3C	4D	5D	6C				
7B	8B	9A	10B	11C	12D	13B	14C	15B	16A
17A	18D	19C	20C	21D	22C	23D	24A	25B	26B
27C	28D	29C	30A	31B	32A	33D	34B	35D	36B
37A	38B	39D	40D	41A	42A	43B	44A,D	45A	
46B	47C	48D	49A,	D50	B51	A,D	52B		

*Lease is another name of Mortgage *All properties in the UK have electricity supplied at 240 volts. If only one person lives in the flat or house, you get a 25% reduction on your Council Tax. *(This does not apply in Northern Ireland).

(1) Who resides at 10, Downing Street, in London?
   A. The Prime Minister   B. the Archbishop of Canterbury
   C. the London's MP   D. The Chancellor of the Exchequer

(2) What is the title of the Minister responsible for law, order and immigration?
   A. The Chancellor of the Exchequer   B. The Home Secretary
   C. The Secretary of Law   D. Minister of Interior

(3) Who wrote the United Kingdom's constitution?
   A. King George III   B. Queen Victoria
   C. Nobody, it's an unwritten constitution   D. Winston Churchill

(4) What is the Queen's Speech?
   A. The speech that the Queen reads from the Throne in the Buckingham Palace, stating her views and opinions on current political and economical matters
   B. The speech written by the Prime Minister, but read by the Queen, at the beginning of every year, containing the best wishes to the British people
   C. The name of the British Constitution
   D. The speech that the Queen reads every year at the beginning of a new parliamentary session, stating Government's policies for the next session

(5) Who is the heir to the throne?
   A. The Queen's oldest grand-son, Prince William   B. The Queen's husband, Prince Philip
   C. The Prime Minister   D. The Queen's son, Prince of Wales

(6) Where are the headquarters of the Metropolitan Police?
   A. 10 Downing Street   B. Oxford Circus
   C. New Scotland Yard   D. Regent Street

(7) What are the key features of the civil service?
   A. political partisanship and efficiency   B. political neutrality and professionalism
   C. corruption and favouritism   D. independence and efficiency

(8) What are the local governments responsible for?
   A. fire service   B. defence
   C. relations with other countries   D. the exchange rate of the Pound Sterling

(9) What are "pressure groups"?
   A. organisations that try to influence government policy
   B. organisations that try to influence the Queen's position on some issues
   C. organisations that try to sabotage elections
   D. organisations that promote political parties

(10) Queen Elisabeth II has reigned since
   A. 1962   B. 1952
   C. 1972   D. 1982

(11) What is "operational independence", related to the Police?
   A. Government can instruct the Police to arrest any individual
   B. Government is absolutely not involved into the Police affairs
   C. Government cannot instruct the Police to arrest or proceed against any individual
   D. Police is independent from the Government except during special operations

(12) Other constitutional monarchies exist in
   A. France, Austria, Greece   B. Finland, Iceland, Portugal
   C. Ireland, Switzerland, Italy   D. Denmark, Netherlands, Norways, Spain, Sweden

(13) How often are the elections held in Britain?
   A. Every 7 years   B. Every 4 years
   C. Every 3 years   D. At least every 5 years

(14) Who defends the debating rights of the Opposition in the Parliament?
   A. The Hansard   B. The Prime Minister   C. The Speaker   D. The Queen

*CV is Curriculum Vita that gives details of Education, Qualifications, previous employment skills. Covering Letter is a short letter attached to a completed application form.
*your speed limit on built up area is 30 mph

Chapter 4 Practice Exam

45

Chapter 4

(15) Who are the Whips?
   A. Leaders of parliamentary committees
   B. A small group of MPs, appointed by their party leaders, to ensure discipline and attendance of MPs at voting time
   C. Speaker's assistants
   D. People who hold the Queen's speech while she is reading it

(16) In the elections, what is the "first past the post" system?
   A. The candidate who gains more votes than any other is elected, even if he or she does not have a majority of the total votes cast
   B. The candidate who has the majority of the total votes cast, is elected
   C. The candidate that gets more than 50% of all votes is elected
   D. The candidate that gets more than 3/4 of all votes is elected

(17) The Scottish Parliament
   A. may pass legislation on anything not specifically reserved to the UK Parliament
   B. may pass laws on defense and foreign affairs
   C. may pass laws on general economic policy
   D. is not elected by a form of proportional representation

(18) If resident in the UK, Canadian and German citizens can vote in national parliamentary elections in the UK
   A. Germans, but not Canadians   B. Canadians, but not Germans   C. True
   D. False, only British citizens can elect National Parliament

(19) Elections for local government councillors are held each year in
   A. February   B. March   C. May   D. April

(20) The Speaker of the House of Commons is
   A. is an MP that has been reelected at least 3 times
   B. is an MP that has been Chief Whip for at least 3 years
   C. is an MP selected by the Queen
   D. an ordinary MP

(21) How many countries are members of the European Union?
   A. 13   B. 15   C. 20   D. 27

(22) When did Britain join the European Economic Community?
   A. in 1968   B. in 1982   C. in 1973   D. in 1988

(23) The European Convention on Human Rights was drawn up by the
   A. European Union
   B. Council of Europe
   C. European Economic Community
   D. European Commission

(24) The European Parliament meets in
   A. Strasbourg   B. Brussels   C. Berlin   D. Luxembourg

*Social security is a welfare benefits to people who do not have enough money to live
*Housing benefit is given if you need help to pay your rent if you are on low income.
*EMA is Education maintenance allowance given to you to help your studies

(25) What organisation is the civil service of the European Union?
   A. The European Commission
   B. The Council of Europe
   C. The European Government
   D. The European Bureau

(26) Which country is part of the Commonwealth?
   A. USA   B. South Africa
   C. Norway   D. Panama

(27) What international organization is working to prevent war and to maintain international peace?
   A. UNESCO   B. UNICEF
   C. United Nations Organization   D. Red Cross

(28) The UK is permanent member of the Security Council of which international organization?
   A. UNICEF   B. UNESCO   C. Red Cross   D. UN

(29) Citizens of EU countries can travel to any EU country as long as they have a valid Passport or Identity Card, and this right cannot be restricted.
   A. False. A visa is also required for some EU states.
   B. True.
   C. This right can be restricted for reasons of public security.
   D. This right can be restricted for reasons of public health, public order and public security.

(30) Britain was one of the founder members of
   A. The European Union (then called European Economic Community, EEC)
   B. The European Parliament
   C. The Council of Europe
   D. The Shenguen Agreement

31 A judge can order a public body to change its practicesor pay compensation if it is not respecting a person's human rights. Is this statement true or false?
   A True   B False

32 Everyone in the UK has the legal right to practise the religion of their choice. Is this statement true or false?
   A True   B False

33 What must a candidate achieve in order to win their constituency?
   A Be a member of the party that wins government office
   B Win at least 15,000 votes
   C Win at least 25% of the votes within their constituency
   D Win the most votes out of all candidates in their constituency

34 What is the current minimum age for standing for public office?
   A 18 years   B 21 years   C 25 years   D 30 years

35 What Is the name of the largest police force in the United Kingdom?
   A AHumberside Police
   B Merseyside Police
   C The Bill
   D The Metropolitan Police

36 A judge can decide whether a person is guilty or innocent of a serious crime. Is this statement true or false?
   A True   B False

*If you have to leave your job because the life has made difficult for you at work or you are dismissed unfairly form work *If you lose your job because the company no longer needs you or cannot afford to pay you may be entitled to a payment called redungancy pay

Chapter 4

37 The Council of Ministers, together with the European Parliament is the legislative body of the European Union. Is this statement true or false/
 A True B False

38 What is a Life Peer?
 A A hereditary aristocrat or peer of the realm
 B A member of the House of Lords who has been appointed by the Prime Minister
 C Any person who has inherited a peerage from II
 D Any person who has served as an MP for more than twenty years

39 In which year were the Assembly for Wales .UK! the Scottish Parliament created?
 A 1969   B 1972   C1982   D 1999

40 Whore is th Commission
 A Brussels   B Geneva   C Paris   D Strasbourg

41 In what year did the Prime Minister gain powers to nominate members of the House of Lords?
 A1958   B1968   C 1973   D 1980

42   What is the name of the ministerial position that is responsible for the economy?
 A Chancellor of the Exchequer
 B Chief Whip
 C Home Secretary
 D Lord Chancellor

43 Who is responsible for investigating serious complaints against the police?
 A The Home Secretary
 B The Independent Police Complaints Commission
 C The Lord Chancellor
 D The Police Commissioner

44 On which matters can the Scottish Parliament make decisions? Select two options from below
 A Education   B Foreign Policy   C Defence   D Health

45 Where does the Scottish Parliament sit?
 A Aberdeen   B Edinburgh   C Glasgow   D Stormont

46 How many Members of the Scottish Parliament (MSPs) are there?
 A 105   B 129   C 158   D 97

47 Where "is "the National Assembly for Wales situated?
 A Cardiff   B Edinburgh   C Stormont   D Swansea

48 How many Assembly Members are there in the National Assembly for Wales?
 A About 30 members   B About 40 members
 C About 50 members   D About 60 members

49 On which matters can the Welsh Assembly make decisions? Select two options from below
 A Transport   B Foreign Policy   C Defence   D Environment

50 The UK government cannot suspend the Northern Ireland Assembly. Is this statement true or false?
 A True   B False

51 On which matters can the Northern Ireland Assembly make decisions? Select two options from below
 A Education   B Foreign Policy   C Defence   D Environment

52 The Northern Ireland Assembly was established with a power-sharing agreement between the main political parties. Is this statement true or false?
 A True   B False

 *Your speed on motorway is 70 mph
 *National insurance contributions pay for retirement pensions and the NHS
 *Tax is contributed towards education army road etc

48

Housing ہاؤسنگ (گھر)

Two-thirds of people in the UK own their own home. Most other people rent houses, flats or rooms.

2/3 حصہ لوگوں کا اپنا گھر ہے اور زیادہ تر لوگ کرائے پر رہتے ہیں۔

Mortgage, a special loan from a bank or building society. This loan is paid back, with interest over a long period of time, usually 25 years

مارگیج ایک خاص لون ہے جو لوگ بینک سے یا بلڈنگ سوسائٹی سے لیتے ہیں جو کہ عام طور پر 25 سال میں انٹرسٹ کے ساتھ واپس کرنا ہوتا ہے۔

If you are having problems paying your mortgage repayments, you can get help and advice. It is important to speak to your bank or building society as soon as you can.

اگر آپ کو مارگیج واپس کرنے میں کوئی پریشانی ہے تو آپ بینک سے یا بلڈنگ سوسائٹی سے مشورہ لے سکتے ہیں اور جتنی جلدی ہو سکے بینک کو بتائیں۔

If you wish to buy a home, usually the first place to start is an estate agent. In Scotland the process is different and you should go to a solicitor first

جب آپ گھر خریدنا چاہیں تو آپ سب سے پہلے اسٹیٹ ایجنٹ کے پاس جاتے ہیں۔ لیکن سکاٹ لینڈ میں آپ پہلے سولیسٹر کے پاس جاتے ہیں

Estate agents represent the person selling their house or flat. They arrange for buyers to visit homes that are for sale.

اسٹیٹ ایجنٹ ان افراد کی نمائندگی کرتے ہیں جو اپنا گھر یا فلیٹ بیچنا چاہتے ہیں اور جس نے گھر خریدنا ہوتا ہے اسے گھر دکھاتے ہیں۔

In the UK, except in Scotland, when you find a home you wish to buy you have to make an offer to the seller. You usually do this through an estate agent or solicitor. Your first offer must be 'subject to contract' so that you can withdraw if there are reasons why you cannot complete the purchase

یو کے میں (سکاٹ لینڈ کے علاوہ) آپ گھر بیچنے والے کو سولیسٹر یا وکیل کے ذریعے آفر دیتے ہیں اور یہ آفر ایک دستاویز ہوتا ہے یعنی آپ اگر کسی وجہ سے نہ خرید سکیں تو دستبردار ہو جائیں۔

In Scotland the seller sets a price and buyers make offers over that amount.

سکاٹ لینڈ میں بیچنے والا آفر دیتا ہے اور خریدار اس کے اوپر آفر دیتا ہے۔

*Key points to remeber in chapter 5

*Mortgage, a special loan from a bank or building society. This loan is paid back, with interest over a long period of time, usually 25 years. The average hourly pay rate for women is 20% less than for men.

49

Chapter 5

It is important that a solicitor helps you through the process of buying a house or flat. When you make an offer on a property, the solicitor will carry out a number of legal checks on the property, the seller and the local area. The solicitor will provide the legal agreements necessary for you to buy the property.

سولیسٹر گھر خریدنے میں آپ کی مدد کرتا ہے۔ جب آپ آفر دیتے ہیں تو سولیسٹر کئی چیزیں چیک کرتا ہے جیسے کہ سیل، لوکل ایریا اور سولیسٹر ضروری کاغذی کاروائی مکمل کرتا ہے۔ جوکہ گھر خریدنے کیلئے ضروری ہوتی ہے

The bank or building society that is providing you with your mortgage will also carry out checks on the house or flat you wish to buy. These are done by a surveyor.

بینک اور بلڈنگ سوسائٹی جو آپ کو قرضہ دیتی ہے وہ بھی گھر کا سروے کرتے ہیں ان کو سرویئر کہتے ہیں۔

In Scotland the survey is carried out before an offer is made, to help people decide how much they want to bid for the property

سکاٹ لینڈ میں سروے آفر دینے سے پہلے کیا جاتا ہے تاکہ لوگ اندازہ لگا سکیں کہ کتنے کی پراپرٹی خریدنی چاہئے

Private property owners called landlords.

پرائیویٹ پراپرٹی رکھنے والوں کو لینڈ لارڈ کہتے ہیں۔

Most local authorities (or councils) provide housing. This is often called council housing. In Northern Ireland social housing is provided by the Northern Ireland Housing Executive

لوکل اتھارٹی (کونسل) کو کونسل ہاؤسنگ بھی کہتے ہیں جو کہ گھر دیتی ہے اور ناردرن آئیرلینڈ میں کونسل کو ہاؤسنگ ایگزیکٹو کہتے ہیں۔

Everyone is entitled to apply for council accommodation. To apply you must put your name on the council register or list.

کونسل کا مکان سب اپلائی کر سکتے ہیں مگر اپلائی کرنے کیلئے آپ کا نام کونسل رجسٹر میں ہونا چاہئے

You have priority and have more points to get council accomodation e.g if you are in chronic ill health, have children, homeless etc

برتری حاصل ہونا مثال کے طور پہ اگر آپ بے گھر ہیں یا پھر پوائنٹ سسٹم اگر آپ کے بچے ہیں آپ بیمار ہیں تو آپ کو زیادہ پوائنٹ ملیں گے۔

It is important to note that in many areas of the UK there is a shortage of council accommodation & that some people have to wait a very long time for a house or flat.

یہ بات نوٹ کریں کہ یو کے میں کونسل کے مکانوں کی کمی ہے اور کچھ لوگوں کو بہت عرصہ انتظار کرنا پڑتا ہے۔

*Two - thirds of people in the UK own their own home. For about 25years, people from the West Indies, India, Pakistan, and later Bangladesh, traveled to work and settle in Britain.

50

Housing associations are independent not-for-profit organisations which provide housing for rent.

ہاؤسنگ ایسوسی ایشن نان پروفٹ ادارے ہوتے ہیں جو گھر کرائے پر دلاتے ہیں۔

'Shared Ownership' which help people buy part of a house or flat if they cannot afford to buy all of it at once.

شیئر آنرشپ کا یہ فائدہ ہے کہ ایک وقت میں پورا گھر نہیں خرید سکتے تو ایک حصہ خرید لیں

Information about **private accmodation** can be found in local newspapers, notice boards, estate agents and letting agents.

پرائیویٹ گھر کے بارے میں انفارمیشن لوکل نیوز پیپر، نوٹس بورڈ، اسٹیٹ ایجنٹ سے معلومات مل سکتی ہیں۔

When you rent a house or flat privately you sign a tenancy agreement, or lease. This explains the conditions or 'rules' you must follow while renting the property.

جب آپ کرائے پہ گھر لیتے ہیں تو کرایہ نامہ پر سائن کرتے ہیں کرایہ نامہ میں شرائط ہوتی ہیں جن پر عمل کرنا ضروری ہوتا ہے۔

A list of any furniture or fittings in the property. This is called an **inventory**.

پراپرٹی میں جو کچھ بھی لگا ہوتا ہے۔ ان کو انوینٹری کہتے ہیں۔

A deposit at the beginning of your tenancy. This is to cover the cost of any damage. It is usually equal to one month's rent. The landlord must return this money to you at the end of your tenancy, unless you have caused damage to the property.

کرایہ شروع ہونے سے پہلے بیانہ دینا ہوتا ہے جو نقصان کی صورت میں ایک مہینے کا کرایہ رکھ لیا جاتا ہے مالک مکان مکان خالی کرنے سے پہلے واپس کر دیتا ہے اگر کرائے دارنے کوئی نقصان نہ کیا ہو۔

Your rent is fixed with your landlord at the beginning of the tenancy. The landlord cannot raise the rent without your agreement. If you have a low income or unemployed you may be able to claim Housing Benefit to help you pay your rent.

آپ کا کرایہ فکس ہوتا ہے اور مالک مکان کرایہ بغیر ایگریمنٹ کے نہیں بڑھا سکتا۔ اگر آپ کی آمدنی کم ہو یا آپ بے روزگار ہوں تو آپ ہاؤسنگ فوائد لے سکتے ہیں

Your tenancy agreement will be for a fixed period of time, often six months. After this time the tenancy can be ended or, if both tenant and landlord agree, renewed. If you **end the tenancy** before the fixed time, you usually have to pay the rent for the agreed full period of the tenancy.

آپ کا ایگریمنٹ عام طور پر چھے ماہ تک کا ہوتا ہے اس کے بعد اگر دونوں چاہیں تو رینیو کرا لیں یا ختم کر دیں۔ اگر آپ فکس ایگریمنٹ سے پہلے مکان خالی کرنا چاہیں تو پھر بھی آپ کو جب تک ایگریمنٹ ہے تب تک کرایہ دینا پڑے گا۔

Chapter 5 Everyday Needs

51

Chapter 5

A landlord cannot force a tenant to leave. If a landlord wishes a tenant to leave they must follow the correct procedures. It is a criminal offence for a landlord to use threats or violence against a tenant or to force them to leave without an order from court.

لینڈ لارڈ ٹیننٹ کو باہر نہیں نکال سکتا اگر مالک نکالنا چاہتا ہے تو اس کیلئے ایک سسٹم ہے۔ کورٹ آرڈر کے بغیر کرایہ دار کو نکالنا یا دھمکی دینا جرم ہے۔

It is unlawful for a landlord to discriminate against someone looking for accommodation because of their sex, race, nationality, or ethnic group, or because they are disabled, unless the landlord or a close relative of the landlord is sharing the accommodation.

یہ جرم ہے کہ کسی کو کمتر سمجھنے کی وجہ سے مکان نہ دینا جیسے کسی معذور کو یا کسی اور مذہب سے تعلق کی وجہ سے مکان نہ دینا سوائے اس صورت میں کہ مالک یا اس کا قریبی اسی گھر میں رہ رہا ہو۔

If you are homeless you should go for help to the local authority (or, in Northern Ireland, the Housing Executive). They have a legal duty to offer help and advice, but will not offer you a place to live unless you have priority need and have a connection with the area, such as work or family. You must also show that you have not made yourself intentionally homeless.

اگر آپ بے گھر ہو جائیں تو آپ لوکل اتھارٹی کے پاس جائیں وہ آپ کی مدد کریں گے مگر گھر نہیں دیں گے جب تک کہ آپ کو برتری نہ حاصل ہو اور آپ کا لوکل علاقے سے کوئی واسطہ ہو ۔ اور آپ کو یہ بھی ثابت کرنا ہوتا ہے کہ آپ نے جان بوجھ کر اپنے آپ کو بے گھر تو نہیں کیا۔

The housing department of the local authority will give advice on homelessness and on Housing Benefit as well as deal with problems you may have in council owned property.

لوکل اتھارٹی کا ہاؤسنگ کا شعبہ آپ کو بے گھر ہونے پر مشورے دیتا ہے اور کونسل کی پراپرٹی کے مسائل میں مدد کرتا ہے

The charge for this is called the water rates. When you move in to a new home (bought or rented), you should receive a letter telling you the name of the company responsible for supplying your water. The water rates may be paid in one payment (a lump sum) or in instalments, usually monthly. If you receive Housing Benefit, you should check to see if this covers the water rates.

پانی کے بل کو واٹر ریٹ کہتے ہیں۔ جب آپ نئے گھر میں جاتے ہیں تو پانی کی کمپنی بل بھیجتی ہے ۔ واٹر بل لم سم ادا کر سکتے ہیں یا پھر ماہانہ قسطوں میں ۔ اگر آپ ہاؤسنگ فوائد لیتے ہیں تو یہ دیکھنا چاہئے کہ پانی کا بل بھی شامل ہے کہ نہیں

*Over the last 20 years, family patterns in Britain have been transformed because of changing attitudes towards divorce and separation *86% of young people had taken part in some form of community event over the past year, and 50% had taken part in fund -raising or collecting money for charity. England (84% of the population) 50.1 million *Shelter Is a Housing Charity

52

In Northern Ireland water is currently (2006) included in the domestic rates,

ناردرن آئرلینڈ میں پانی کے بل کو ڈومیسٹک ریٹ کہتے ہیں۔

All properties in the UK have electricity supplied at 240 volts. Most homes also have gas. When you move into a new home or leave an old one, you should make a note of the electricity and gas meter readings.

یوکے میں بجلی 240 وولٹ کی سپلائی دی جاتی ہے۔ زیادہ گھروں میں گیس ہے۔ جب پرانا گھر چھوڑتے ہیں یا نئے گھر میں جاتے ہیں تو آپ کو بجلی اور گیس میٹر ریڈنگ نوٹ کرنی چاہئے۔

company supplies your gas) is Transco

گیس سپلائی کرنے والی کمپنی کا نام ٹرانسکو ہے۔

company supplies your electricity is Energywatch

بجلی سپلائی کرنے والی کمپنی کا نام اینرجی واچ ہے۔

Telephone line(called a land line). (company supply you telephone is Ofcom)

ٹیلیفون لائن کو لینڈ لائن کہتے ہیں اور سپلائی کرنے والی کمپنی کو آف کام کہتے ہیں۔

Dial 999 or 112 for emergency calls for police, fire or ambulance service. These calls are free

999 اور 112 ایمرجنسی پولیس، آگ اور ایمبولینس کیلئے ہے

Information on how to pay for water, gas, electricity and the telephone is found on the back of each bill. If you have a bank account you can pay your bills by standing order or direct debit.

پانی، بجلی، گیس اور ٹیلیفون کے بل کی معلومات بل کے پچھلے صفحے پر درج ہوتی ہیں۔ اگر آپ کا بنک اکاؤنٹ ہے تو ڈائریکٹ ڈیبٹ سے بل جمع کرا سکتے ہیں۔

If you do not pay a bill, the service can be cutoff. To get a service reconnected, you have to pay another charge.

اگر آپ بل جمع نہ کرائیں تو کنکشن کٹ جاتا ہے۔ اور بحال کرنے کیلئے فائن دینا پڑتا ہے۔

Refuse is also called waste, or rubbish. The local authority collects the waste regularly, usually on the same day of each week. Waste must be put outside in a particular place to get collected

ریفیوز کو ویسٹ بھی کہتے ہیں۔ لوکل اتھارٹی ہر ہفتے سیم ڈے کچرا اٹھاتے ہیں۔ کچرا ایک خاص جگہ پہ رکھنا چاہے۔

UK population 2001
Prescriptions are free for anyone who is: under 16 years of age (under 25 in Wales) under 19 and in full-time education aged 60 or over

Chapter 5 Everyday Needs

53

Chapter 5

Large objects which you want to throw away, such as a bed, a wardrobe or a fridge, need to be collected separately. Contact the local authority to arrange this. If you have a business, such as a factory or a shop, you must make special arrangements with the local authority for your waste to be collected. It is a criminal offence to dump rubbish anywhere.

بیڈ، الماری، فرج وغیرہ کی سپیشل کلیکشن ہوتی ہے آپ فون کر کے کروا سکتے ہیں۔ اگر آپ کا بزنس ہے تو آپ لوکل اتھارٹی سے رابطہ کریں کہ وہ کچرا اکٹھا کریں۔ کسی بھی جگہ کچرا پھینکنا جرم ہے۔

Local government services, such as education, police, roads, refuse collection and libraries, are paid for partly by grants from the government and partly by Council Tax

لوکل گورنمنٹ سروس، جیسے پولیس، روڈ، کچرا اٹھانے والے، لائبریری وغیرہ کے اخراجات گورنمنٹ ادا کرتی ہے اور کچھ پیسے کونسل ٹیکس سے جاتا ہے۔

In Northern Ireland there is a system of domestic rates instead of the Council Tax.

نادرن آئرلینڈ میں کونسل ٹیکس کو ڈومیسٹک ریٹ کہتے ہیں۔

The amount of Council Tax you pay depends on the size and value of your house or flat (dwelling). You must register to pay Council Tax when you move into a new property, either as the owner or the tenant. You can pay the tax in one payment, in two instalments, or in ten instalments (from April to January)

کونسل ٹیکس کتنا دینا ہے یہ پراپرٹی پر ہوتا ہے کہ کس قسم کی پراپرٹی ہے۔ جب بھی نئی پراپرٹی میں جائیں تو لازمی کونسل ٹیکس دینے کیلئے رجسٹر ہوں چاہے آپ مالک ہوں یا کرائے دار ۔ آپ ٹیکس ایک انسٹالمنٹ میں یا دو یا دس قسطوں میں دے سکتے ہیں۔

If only one person lives in the flat or house, you get a 25% reduction on your Council Tax. (This does not apply in Northern Ireland). You may also get a reduction if someone in the property has a disability. People on a low income or who receive benefits such as Income Support or Jobseeker's Allowance can get Council Tax Benefit.

اگر گھر میں ایک ہی فرد رہتا ہے تو کونسل ٹیکس پر 25% ڈسکاؤنٹ ملتا ہے۔ لیکن ناردرن آئرلینڈ میں ایسا نہیں ہوتا۔ اگر گھر میں کوئی معذور ہو تو بھی ٹیکس میں کمی ہوتی ہے۔ جن کی تنخواہ کم ہو یا جو انکم سپورٹ پر ہیں ان کو کونسل ٹیکس بینفٹ ملتے ہیں۔

*General population in the UK has increased in the last 20 years *There are more people over 60 than children under 16 *There is also a record number of people aged 85 and over *The census information remains confidential and anonymous; *it can only be released to the public after 100 years.

You can get advice on this from the local authority or the Citizens Advice Bureau.

آپ لوکل اتھارٹی یا سٹیزن ایڈوائس بیورو سے مشورے لے سکتے ہیں۔

If you buy a home with a mortgage, you must insure the building against fire, theft and accidental damage. The landlord should arrange insurance for rented buildings.

اگر آپ مارگیج پہ گھر لیتے ہیں تو آپ کو لازمی ہر قسم کے حادثے کی انشورنس کروانی پڑتی ہے۔ کرائے پر مکان کی انشورنس مالک مکان کراتا ہے۔

If you do have problems with your neighbours, they can usually be solved by speaking to them first. If you cannot solve the problem, speak to your landlord, local authority or housing association.

اگر آپ کا پڑوسیوں کے ساتھ مسئلہ ہے تو عام طور پر ان سے بات کر کے حل ہو جاتا ہے اگر پھر بھی حل نہیں ہوتا تو اپنے مالک مکان سے بات کریں، لوکل اتھارٹی یا ہاؤسنگ ایسوسی ایشن سے بات کریں۔

Neighbours who cause a very serious nuisance may be taken to court and can be evicted from their home.

ایسے پڑوسی جو بہت ٹربل کرتے ہیں ان کو کورٹ کے ذریعے نکالا جا سکتا ہے۔

There are several mediation organisations which help neighbours to solve their disputes without having to go to court. Mediators talk to both sides and try to find a solution acceptable to both.

کئی ادارے ہیں جو نمبرز کے مسائل حل کرنے میں مدد کرتے ہیں میڈی ایٹرز دونوں کی باتیں سنتے ہیں اور کورٹ میں جائے بغیر مسئلے کا حل نکال لیتے ہیں۔

Bank notes in the UK come in denominations (values) of £5, £10, £20 and £50. Northern Ireland and Scotland have their own bank notes which are valid everywhere in the UK,

بینک کے نوٹ انگلینڈ میں 5,10،20،50 کے ملتے ہیں۔ ناردرن آئرلینڈ اور سکاٹ لینڈ کے اپنے نوٹ ہیں جو کہ انگلینڈ میں بھی چلتے ہیں۔

In January 2002 twelve European Union (EU) states adopted the euro as their common currency

جنوری 2002 میں بارہ ملکوں نے یورو کرنسی اختیار کی

British people vote for the euro in a referendum.

برٹش لوگ ریفرنڈم کے ذریعے یورو اختیار کرنے کا فیصلہ کریں گے۔

The euro does circulate to some extent in Northern Ireland, particularly in the towns near the border with Ireland.

یورو ناردرن آئرلینڈ کے کچھ بارڈر کے علاقوں میں چلتا ہے۔

*Free dental treatment is available to:-
People under 18 (in Wales people under 25 and over 60) _ pregnant women and women with babies under 12 months old. *People on income support, Jobseekers' Allowance or Pension Credit Guarantee

Chapter 5 Everyday Needs

55

Chapter 5

You can get or change foreign currency at banks, building societies, large post offices and exchange shops or bureaux de change.

فارن کرنسی آپ بینک سے، پوسٹ آفس سے، اور بیورکس دے ایکسچینج سے چینج کروا سکتے ہیں۔

To open an account you need to show documents to prove your identity, such as a passport, immigration document or driving licence. You also need to show something with your address on it like a tenancy agreement or household bill.

بینک اکاؤنٹ کھولنے کیلئے آپ کو آئی ڈی دینی ہوتی ہے جیسے کہ پاسپورٹ، ویزا یا ڈرائیونگ لائسنس۔ آپ کو اپنی رہائش کا بھی ثبوت دینا ہوتا ہے جیسے کہ بل وغیرہ

Cash cards allow you to use cash machines to withdraw money from your account. For this you need a Personal Identification Number (PIN), which you must keep secret. A debit card allows you to pay for things without using cash. You must have enough money in your account to cover what you buy. If you lose your cash card or debit card you must inform the bank immediately.

کیش کارڈ سے مشین سے پیسے نکال سکتے ہیں اس کیلئے آپ کو پن نمبر چاہئے ہوتا ہے۔ ڈیبٹ کارڈ سے بغیر پیسوں کے آپ چیزیں خرید سکتے ہیں۔ اس کیلئے آپ کے بینک میں اتنے پیسے ہونے چاہئیں جتنے کی آپ نے شاپنگ کرنی ہے

Credit cards can be used to buy things in shops, on the telephone and over the internet. A store card is like a credit card but used only in a specific shop. Credit and store cards do not draw money from your bank account but you will be sent a bill every month. If you do not pay the total amount on the bill, you are charged interest.

کریڈٹ کارڈ سے آپ آن لائن یا ٹیلیفون پر شاپنگ کر سکتے ہیں۔ سٹور کارڈ کریڈٹ کارڈ کی طرح ہوتا ہے لیکن صرف سٹور میں ہی یوز ہو سکتا ہے۔ کریڈٹ کارڈ اور سٹور کارڈ بینک سے پیسے نہیں نکال سکتے اور جو شاپنگ کرتے ہیں اس کا بل گھر آجاتا ہے۔ اگر آپ بل وقت پر ادا نہ کریں تو آپ کو فائن دینا پڑتا ہے۔

If you lose your credit or store cards you must inform the company immediately.

اگر آپ کا کریڈٹ کارڈ یا سٹور کارڈ گم ہو جائے تو اپنی کمپنی کو فوری اطلاع دیں۔

People in the UK often borrow money from banks and other organisations to pay for things like household goods, cars and holidays.

یو کے میں لوگ بینک سے لون لیتے ہیں تا کہ وہ بل دے سکیں گاڑی لیں اور چھٹیوں پہ جا سکیں۔

*Pregnant or with a baby under 12 months old
*Suffering from a specified medical condition. _ receiving Income Support, Jobseekers'
*Allowance, Working. Families or Disabilities Tax Credit

Chapter 5 Everyday Needs

Banks make a decision about a loan, such as your occupation, address, salary and previous credit record. If you apply for a loan you might be refused. If this happens, you have the right to ask the reason why.

بینک آپ کو لون دینے یا نہ دینے کا فیصلہ آپ کے کام، رہائش اور کریڈٹ ریکارڈ سے کرتا ہے اگر آپ لون اپلائی کریں تو آپ کا لون ریفیوز بھی ہوسکتا ہے۔ اگر ایسا ہو تو آپ پوچھ سکتے ہیں کہ کیوں ریفیوز کیا ہے

Credit unions are financial co-operatives owned and controlled by their members. The members pool their savings and then make loans from this pool. Interest rates in credit unions are usually lower than banks and building societies.

کریڈٹ یونین فنانس کو پرائیویٹ ہوتی ہے اور اس کو ممبر چلاتے ہیں اور کنٹرول کرتے ہیں اور سب مل کر سیونگ کرتے ہیں اور پھر ممبر کو لون دیتے ہیں۔ ان کا انٹرسٹ ریٹ بینک سے کم ہوتا ہے

Insurance is compulsory if you have a car or motorcycle.

کار اور موٹر سائیکل کی انشورنس کرانا ضروری ہوتا ہے۔

The UK has a system of social security which pays welfare benefits to people who do not have enough money to live on. Benefits are usually available for the sick and disabled, older people, the unemployed and those on low incomes. People who do not have legal rights of residence (or 'settlement') in the UK cannot usually receive benefits.

سوشل سیکیورٹی ان لوگوں کو ملتا ہے جن کے پاس گزارا کرنے کیلئے پیسے نہیں ہوتے۔ اور بینیفٹ ان لوگوں کو ملتا ہے جو بیمار ہیں معذور ہیں، بے روزگار یا کم آمدنی والے ہیں۔

Healthcare in the UK is organised under the National Health Service (NHS). The NHS began in 1948, and is one of the largest organisations in Europe. It provides all residents with free healthcare and treatment.

ہیلتھ کی انتظامیہ NHS ہے۔ یہ 1948 میں شروع ہوا اور یورپ کا سب سے بڑا ادارہ ہے۔ اس کا کام تمام لوگوں کو مفت علاج مہیا کرنا ہے۔

Family doctors are called General Practitioners (GPs) and they work in surgeries. GPs often work together in a group practice. This is sometimes called a Primary Health Care Centre.

فیملی ڈاکٹر کو جی پی کہتے ہیں جو کہ سرجری میں کام کرتے ہیں۔ جہاں کچھ جی پی مل کر کام کرتے ہیں تو ان کو پرائمری ہیلتھ کیئر سینٹر کہتے ہیں۔

*Pdsa people's dispensary for sick animals *Pals patient advice and liaison service
Ipcc independent police complaint commission *Naric national academic recognized international centre.

Chapter 5

Your GP is responsible for organising the health treatment you receive. Treatment can be for physical and mental illnesses. If you need to see a specialist, you must go to your GP first. Your GP will then refer you to a specialist in a hospital

آپ کا جی پی آپ کی ہیلتھ جسمانی یا ذہنی کا ذمہ دار ہوتا ہے۔ اگر آپ سپیشلسٹ کو ملنا چاہتے ہیں تو پہلے جی پی سے بات کریں۔ آپ کا جی پی سپیشلسٹ کو ریفر کریگا۔

You can attend a hospital without a GP's letter only in the case of an emergency. If you have an emergency you should go to the Accident and Emergency (A & E)

آپ ہسپتال اسی صورت میں جاسکتے ہیں جب آپ کے پاس جی پی کا لیٹر ہو یا پھر ایمرجنسی ہو۔ ایمرجنسی میں آپ A&E جاتے ہیں۔

You should look for a GP as soon as you move to a new area.

جب بھی آپ نئے علاقے میں جائیں فوری طور پر جی پی سے رجسٹر ہوں

medical card. If you do not have one, the GP's receptionist should give you a form to send to the local health authority.

آپ کو میڈیکل کارڈ حاصل کرنے کیلئے جی پی کی ریسپشن سے ایک فارم فل کرکے دینا ہوتا ہے جو کہ لوکل اتھارٹی کو دینا ہوتا ہے۔

If you cannot find a GP, you can ask your local health authority to help you find one.

اگر آپ کو جی پی نہیں ملتا تو لوکل ہیلتھ اتھارٹی سے پوچھیں

All patients registering with a GP are entitled to a free health check.

Appointments to see the GP can be made by phone or in person. Sometimes you might have to wait several days before you can see a doctor. If you need immediate medical attention ask for an urgent appointment.

جو بھی جی پی سے رجسٹر ہوتا ہے اس کا فری چیک اپ ہوتا ہے۔ جی پی سے اپائنٹمنٹ فون پر یا جا کر بنا سکتے ہیں۔ کبھی کبھی کافی دن کا انتظار کرنا پڑتا ہے اگر آپ کو جلدی ہے تو ارجنٹ بنالیں۔

If you have asked for an interpreter, it is important that you keep your appointment because this service is expensive.

اگر آپ نے انٹرپریٹر کا بھی انتظام کیا ہے تو لازمی جائیں کیونکہ یہ سروس مہنگی ہوتی ہے۔

In exceptional circumstances, GPs can visit patients at home but they give priority to people who are unable to travel.

سنگین حالات میں ڈاکٹر گھر بھی جاتے ہیں لیکن برتری ان کو ملتی ہے جو سفر نہ کر سکیں

*Most people have to pay for sight tests and glasses, except children, people over 60, people with certain eye conditions and people receiving certain benefits *In Scotland, eye tests are free.
*Your must register your baby with the Registrar of Births, Marriages and Deaths (Register Office) within six weeks of the birth.

Treatment from the GP is free but you have to pay a charge for your medicines and for certain services, such as vaccinations for travel abroad.

جی پی سے علاج فری ہے مگر دوائی کے پیسے آپ کو دینے پڑتے ہیں اسی طرح سروسز جیسے ویکسین لگوانے کے پیسے دینے پڑتے ہیں

Prescriptions are free for anyone who is: دوائیاں ان لوگوں کیلیے فری ہیں

- under 16 years of age (under 25 in Wales)
- under 19 and in full-time education
- aged 60 or over
- pregnant or with a baby under 12 months old
- suffering from a specified medical condition   کسی خاص قسم کی مرض میں بتلا ہے
- receiving Income Support, Jobseekers' Allowance, Working Families or Disabilities Tax Credit

If you need minor tests at a hospital, you will probably attend the Outpatients department. If your treatment takes several hours, you will go into hospital as a day patient. If you need to stay overnight, you will go into hospital as an in-patient

اگر آپ نے چھوٹا موٹا علاج کرانا ہے تو آپ آؤٹ پیشنٹ ڈیپارٹمنٹ جاتے ہیں۔ اگر آپ کا علاج کئی گھنٹوں کا ہے تو آپ ڈے پیشنٹ ہیں۔ اگر آپ رات رکیں تو آپ ان پیشنٹ ہیں۔

You will receive all your meals while you are an in-patient   آپ کو کھانا ملے گا اگر آپ ان پیشنٹ ہیں

Patient Advice and Liaison Service (PALS)   مریضوں کو مشوروں کی سروس کو پالز کہتے ہیں

Most people have to pay for dental treatment   زیادہ تر لوگوں کو دانتوں کے علاج کے پیسے دینے پڑتے ہیں

PG (parental guidance): suitable for everyone but some parts of the film might be unsuitable for children. 12 or 12A: Children under 12 are not allowed to see or rent the film unless they are with an adult. 15: Children under 15 are not allowed to see or rent the film.

Chapter 5

Free dental treatment is available to
☐ people under 18 (in Wales people under 25 and over 60) 61
☐ pregnant women and women with babies under 12 months old
☐ People on income support, Jobseekers' Allowance or Pension Credit

Most people have to pay for sight tests and glasses, except children, people over 60, people with certain eye conditions and people receiving certain benefits. In Scotland, eye tests are free

زیادہ تر لوگوں کو آنکھوں کے علاج کے پیسے دینے پڑتے ہیں سوائے بچّوں کے اور ساٹھ سال سے زیادہ عمر کے لوگوں کے یا ان کا فری ہے جو مخصوص آنکھوں کے مرض میں مبتلا ہیں یا وہ لوگ جو بینفٹس لیتے ہیں ۔ سکاٹ لینڈ میں علاج فری ہے ۔

Midwives work in hospitals or health centres. Some GPs do not provide maternity services so you may wish to look for another GP during your pregnancy. In the UK women usually have their babies in hospital,

مڈوائف ہسپتال میں یا ہیلتھ سینٹر میں کام کرتی ہیں کچھ جی پی میٹرنیٹی سروس نہیں دیتے اس لیے پریگنینسی کے دوران کسی اور جی پی سے رابطہ کریں ۔ یو کے میں بچے ہسپتال میں پیدا ہوتے ہیں ۔

A health visitor is a qualified nurse and can advise you about caring for your baby.

ہیلتھ وزیٹر کوالیفائڈ نرس ہوتی ہے اور آپ کے بچے کی دیکھ بھال کے مشورے دیتی ہے ۔

You can ask advice from your health visitor until your child is five years old.

آپ ہیلتھ وزیٹر سے جب تک آپ کا بچہ پانچ سال کا ہوتا ہے مشورے لے سکتے ہیں ۔

The Family Planning Association (FPA) gives advice on contraception and sexual health. The National Childbirth Trust gives information and support in pregnancy, childbirth and early parenthood

فیملی پلاننگ ایسوسی ایشن کو FPA کہتے ہیں جو کنٹراسپشن اور سیکچوئل ہیلتھ کے بارے میں مشورے دیتی ہے نیشنل چائلڈ ٹرسٹ پریگنینسی، بچوں کی پیدائش اور بچوں کو سنبھالنے میں مدد کرتے ہیں ۔

Your must register your baby with the Registrar of Births, Marriages and Death within six weeks of the birth.

برتھ، میرج اور ڈیتھ چھے ہفتوں کے اندر اندر درج کرانا لازمی ہوتا ہے ۔

*Fpa family planning association *EAL English additional language
Ypba young persons bridging allowance
*U (Universal): suitable for anyone aged 4 years and over.

60

If the parents are married, either the mother or father can register the birth. If they are not married, only the mother can register the birth. If the parents are not married but want both names on the child's birth certificate, both mother and father must be present when they register their baby.

اگر پیرنٹس شادی شدہ ہیں تو ماں یا باپ کوئی بھی رجسٹر کرا سکتا ہے اگر وہ میرڈ نہیں ہیں تو صرف ماں رجسٹر کرا سکتی ہے۔ اور اگر دونوں اپنا نام لکھوانا چاہتے ہیں تو دونوں کو حاضر ہونا پڑتا ہے۔

Education in the UK is free and compulsory for all children between the ages of 5 and 16 (4 to 16 in Northern Ireland).

یو کے میں تعلیم فری ہے اور لازمی ہے کہ پانچ سال سے لیکر سولہ سال تک (چار سے سولہ تک نادرن آئرلینڈ میں) اسکول جائیں۔

The child's parent or guardian is responsible for making sure their child goes to school, arrives on time and attends for the whole school year. If they do not do this, the parent or guardian may be prosecuted

بچے کے والدین اس بات کے ذمہ دار ہوتے ہیں کہ بچہ وقت پر اسکول جائے اور سارا سال اسکول حاضر ہے۔ اگر والدین ایسا نہیں کرتے تو ان سے پوچھ گچھ ہو سکتی ہے۔

In England and Wales the primary stage lasts from 5 to 11, in Scotland from 5 to 12 and in Northern Ireland from 4 -11.

انگلینڈ اور ویلز میں پرائمری اسکول پانچ سال سے لیکر گیارہ سال تک ہوتا ہے۔ سکاٹ لینڈ میں پانچ سال سے بارہ سال تک اور نادرن آئرلینڈ میں چار سال سے لیکر گیارہ سال تک ہوتا ہے۔

Secondary schools are larger than primary schools. Most are mixed sex, although there are single sex schools in some areas.

سیکنڈری اسکول پرائمری اسکول سے بڑے ہوتے ہیں۔ زیادہ تر لڑکے لڑکیاں اکٹھا پڑھتے ہیں البتہ صرف لڑکوں کے یا لڑکیوں کے اسکول بھی ہوتے ہیں

Education at state schools in the UK is free, but parents have to pay for school uniforms and sportswear. There are sometimes extra charges for music lessons and for school outings. Parents on low incomes can get help with costs, and with the cost of school meals.

تعلیم تو اسکولوں میں مفت ہے مگر والدین کو یونیفارم اور سپورٹس کے پیسے دینے پڑتے ہیں میوزک لیسن کے پیسے دینے پڑتے ہیں۔ کم آمدنی والوں کو اخراجات میں جیسے اسکول میل میں مدد ملتی ہے

In some areas there are Muslim, Jewish and Sikh schools. In Northern Ireland, some schools are called Integrated Schools. These schools aim to bring children of different religions together. Information on faith schools is available from your local education authority.

کچھ علاقوں میں مسلم، سکھ اور جیوز اسکول ہیں نادرن آئرلینڈ میں کچھ اسکول انٹیگریٹڈ اسکول ہیں جو کہ تمام مذاہب کے بچوں کو پڑھاتے ہیں

*About 8% of children go to independent schools *In Scotland there will soon be a single curriculum for all pupils from age 3 to age 18 *This is called A Curriculum for Excellence *Schools must be open 190 days a year *All parents receive a report every year on their child's progress

Chapter 5 Everyday Needs

61

Chapter 5

Independent schools are private schools. They are not run or paid for by the state. Independent secondary schools are also sometimes called public schools. There are about 2,500 independent schools in the UK. About 8% of children go to these schools. At independent schools parents must pay the full cost of their child's education.

انڈیپنڈنٹ سکول پرائیویٹ سکول ہیں جن کو گورنمنٹ نہیں چلاتی اور نہ ہی پیسے دیتی ہے۔ انڈیپنڈنٹ سیکنڈری سکول کو کبھی کبھی پبلک سکول بھی کہتے ہیں۔ یو کے میں تقریباً 2500 سکول ہیں اور 8% لوگ ان سکولوں میں جاتے ہیں۔

Schools must, by law, provide religious education (RE) to all pupils. Parents are allowed to withdra their children from these lessons.

قانونی طور پہ سکول لازمی مذہبی تعلیم دیں البتہ اگر والدین چاہیں تو اپنے بچے کو کلاس میں نہ بھیجیں۔

All children get careers advice from the age of 14. Advice is also available from Connexions, a national service for young people:

تمام بچوں کو چودہ سال کی عمر میں کیرئیر کے بارے میں مشورے ملتے ہیں اور کونیکشن سے بھی مشورے مل سکتے ہیں۔

A number of places on a school governing body are reserved for parents. The governing body decides how the school is run and administered and produces reports on the progress of the school from year to year

سکول کی گورننگ باڈی میں جگہ ہوتی ہے اگر پیرنٹس چاہیں تو ممبر بن سکتے ہیں گورننگ باڈی فیصلے کرتی ہے کہ سکول کو کیسے چلایا جائے۔ اور سالہا سال کی کیا پروگریس رہی۔

Schools must be open 190 days a year

سکول لازمی 190 دن کھلے رہیں۔

Home-school agreement. This is a list of things that both the school and the parent or guardian agree to do to ensure a good education for the child

ہوم سکول ایگریمنٹ والدین کو سائن کرنا پڑتا ہے تاکہ اچھی تعلیم کی یقین دہانی کرائی جا سکے۔

Most courses are free up to the age of 19. Young people from families with low incomes can get financial help with their studies when they leave school at 16. This is called the Education Maintenance Allowance (EMA)

زیادہ تر کورسز 19 سال تک کی عمر تک فری ہیں جن کی تنخواہ کم ہوتی ہے انہیں سکول چھوڑنے کے بعد EMA ملتا ہے

*18: No one under 18 is allowed to see or rent the film. R18: No one under 18 is allowed to see the film, which is only available in specially licensed cinemas. *Independent secondary schools are also sometimes called public schools. *There are about 2,500 independent schools in the UK.

In Scotland there are no tuition fees but after students finish university they pay back some of the cost of their education in a payment called an endowment. At present, universities can charge up to £3,000 per year for their tuition fees, but students do not have to pay anything towards their fees before or during their studies.

سکاٹ لینڈ میں ٹیوشن فیس نہیں لیکن جب سٹوڈنٹ یونیورسٹی چھوڑتا ہے تو وہ فیس کا کچھ حصہ دیتا ہے جسے اینڈومنٹ کہتے ہیں اس وقت یونیورسٹی کی 3000 پاؤنڈ سالانہ فی ہے لیکن سٹوڈنٹ کو یونیورسٹی سے پہلے یا دوران میں کچھ نہیں دینا پڑتا

The government pays their tuition fees and then charges for them when a student starts working after university. Some families on low incomes receive help with their children's tuition fees. This is called a grant. The universities also give help, in the form of bursaries.

گورنمنٹ ٹیوشن فی دیتی ہے اور جب سٹوڈنٹ کو نوکری ملتی ہے تو گورنمنٹ فیس واپس لیتی ہے کچھ لوگ جن کی آمدنی کم ہوتی ہے ان کو مدد ملتی ہے جسے گرانٹ کہتے ہیں گورنمنٹ برسری کی صورت میں بھی پیسے دیتی ہے۔

Most students get a low - interest student loan from a bank. This pays for their living costs while they are at university

بہت لوگوں کو لو انٹرسٹ لون ملتا ہے جس سے یونیورسٹی کے اخراجات نکلتے ہیں۔

Films in the UK have a system to show if they are suitable for children. This is called the classification system. If a child is below the age of the classification, they should not watch the film at a cinema or on DVD.

یوکے میں فلم کی کلاسیفیکیشن ہوتی ہے کہ بچے دیکھ سکتے ہیں یا نہیں۔

U (Universal): suitable for anyone aged 4 years and over
PG (parental guidance): suitable for everyone but some parts of the film might be unsuitable for children.

سب کیلئے سوٹ ایبل ہے مگر کچھ پارٹ بچے کیلئے نہیں ہیں۔

12 or 12A: Children under 12 are not allowed to see or rent the film unless they are with an adult.

بارہ سال سے کم عمر کے بچے فلم نہیں دے سکتے البتہ ایک بالغ کے ساتھ دیکھ سکتے ہیں

15: Children under 15 are not allowed to see or rent the film.
18: No one under 18 is allowed to see or rent the film.
R18: No one under 18 is allowed to see the film, which is only available in specially licensed cinemas.

کوئی بھی اٹھارہ سال سے کم عمر فلم نہیں دیکھ سکتا اور صرف لائسنس سینما میں دیکھ سکتا ہے۔

*A colour TV license currently costs £131.50 (2006) and lasts for 12 months. People aged 75, or over can apply for a free TV license *Blind people can claim a 50% discount on their TV license.
*Pubs are usually open during the day and until 11p.m. If a pub wants to stay open later, it must apply for a special license.

Chapter 5 Everyday Needs

Chapter 5

Anyone in the UK with a television (TV), DVD or video recorder, computer or any device which is used for watching or recording TV programmes must be covered by a valid television licence. One licence covers all of the equipment at one address, but people who rent different rooms in a shared house must each buy a separate licence.

کوئی بھی ٹی وی یا دیکھنے والی چیز کا لائسنس ہونا ضروری ہے۔ ایک لائسنس ایک گھر کو کور کرتا ہے مگر کرائے پر گھر شیئر کرنے والوں کو الگ الگ لائسنس لینا پڑتا ہے۔

A colour TV licence currently costs £131.50 (2006) and lasts for 12 months. People aged 75, or over can apply for a free TV licence. Blind people can claim a 50% discount on their TV licence. You risk prosecution and a fine if you watch TV but are not covered by a TV licence.

کلر ٹی وی لائسنس کی فیس 131.50 ہے جو کہ ایک سال کیلئے ہوتی ہے۔ 75 سال سے زیادہ عمر کے لوگوں کو فری ٹی وی لائسنس ملتا ہے۔ اندھوں کو 50% ڈسکاؤنٹ ملتا ہے۔ اگر آپ بغیر ٹی وی کے لائسنس دیکھیں تو جرمانہ ہو سکتا ہے۔

National Trust. This is a charity that works to preserve important buildings and countryside in the UK.

نیشنل ٹرسٹ ایک چیریٹی ہے جو کہ اہم عمارات کی اور کنٹری سائڈ کی دیکھ بھال کرتی ہے۔

To drink alcohol in a pub you must be 18 or over. People under 18 are not allowed to buy alcohol in a supermarket or in an off - licence either. The landlord of the pub may allow people of 14 to come into the pub but they are not allowed to drink.

پب میں شراب پینے کی عمر 18 سال ہے۔ اس سے کم عمر کے لوگ شراب نہیں پی سکتے نہ خرید سکتے ہیں اگر لینڈ لارڈ چاہے تو 14 سال کی عمر میں پب میں جا سکتا ہے مگر پی نہیں سکتا۔

At 16, people can drink wine or beer with a meal in a hotel or restaurant. Pubs are usually open during the day and until 11p.m. If a pub wants to stay open later, it must apply for a special licence. Night clubs open and close later than pubs.

سولہ سال کی عمر میں ریسٹورنٹ میں کھانے کے ساتھ شراب پی سکتے ہیں۔ پب عام طور پہ گیارہ بجے تک کھلے ہوتے ہیں اگر زیادہ دیر تک کھلے رکھنے ہیں تو سپیشل لائسنس لینا پڑتا ہے۔ نائٹ کلب رات دیر تک کھلے رہتے ہیں۔

*The cost of their education in a payment called an endowment *Some families on low incomes receive help with their children's tuition fees. This is called a grant *The universities also give help, in the form of bursaries.

64

People under 18 are not allowed into betting shops or gambling clubs.

18 سال سے کم عمر کے لوگ بیٹنگ یا گیمبلنگ شاپ پر نہیں جاسکتے۔

People under 16 are not allowed to buy a lottery ticket or scratch card.

16 سال سے کم عمر کے لوگ لاٹری ٹکٹ یا سکریچ کارڈ نہیں خرید سکتے۔

It is against the law to treat a pet cruelly or to neglect it. All dogs in public places must wear a collar showing the name and address of the owner.

یہ جرم ہے کہ آپ پالتو جانور کا خیال نہ رکھیں پبلک پلیس میں کتے کے پٹے میں مالک کا نام اور پتہ لکھا ہونا چاہئے

Medical treatment for animals are available from veterinary surgeons (vets). If you cannot afford to pay a vet, you can go to a charity called the PDSA (People's Dispensary for Sick Animals).

جانوروں کے بیمار ہونے کی صورت میں آپ ویٹ کو دکھا سکتے ہیں اگر آپ افورڈ نہیں کر سکتے تو pdsa کتوں کی چیریٹی ڈسپینسری میں لے جائیں۔

Usually, tickets for trains and underground systems such as the London Underground must be bought before you get on the train. Discount tickets are available for families, people aged 60 and over, disabled people, students and people under 2 6

ٹرین اور انڈر گراؤنڈ سسٹم جیسے کہ لندن انڈر گراؤنڈ سوار ہونے سے پہلے خریدنی چاہئے۔ فیملی کو، 60 سال سے زائد عمر کو، سٹوڈنٹ کو اور 26 سال سے کم عمر لوگوں کو ڈسکاؤنٹ مل سکتا ہے۔

To operate legally, all taxis and minicabs must be licensed and display a licence plate. Taxis and cabs with no licence are not insured for fare-paying passengers and are not always safe. Women should not use unlicensed minicabs

قانونی طور پر ٹیکسی چلانے کیلئے لائسنس ہونا چاہئے اور ڈسپلے پلیٹ لگانی چاہئے لائسنس کے بغیر ٹیکسی انشور نہیں ہوتی اور سیف نہیں ہوتی۔ خواتین کو بلا لائسنس ٹیکسی میں بھیٹنا نہیں چاہئے۔

You must be at least 17 to drive a car or motorcycle, 18 to drive a medium sized lorry, and 21 to drive a large lorry or bus. To drive a lorry, minibus or bus with more than eight passenger seats, you must have a special licence.

کار یا موٹر سائیکل چلانے کیلئے آپ کی عمر 17 سال ہونی چاہئے 18 سال کی عمر میں آپ میڈیم سائز گاڑی چلا سکتے ہیں 21 سال کی عمر میں بڑی لاری چلا سکتے ہیں اور آپ کو سپیشل لائسنس لینا پڑتا ہے جس میں آٹھ افراد بیٹھ سکتے ہیں۔

Chapter 5 Everyday Needs

65

Chapter 5

If your driving licence is from a country in the European Union (EU), Iceland, Liechtenstein or Norway, you can drive in the UK for as long as your licence is valid. You must have a driving licence to drive on public roads.

اگر آپ کا لائسنس یورپین یونین سے ہے تو جب تک آپ کا لائسنس ویلڈ ہے آپ گاڑی چلا سکتے ہیں۔

Provisional licence. You need this licence while you are learning to drive. With this you are allowed to drive a motorcycle up to 125cc or a car. You must put L plates on the vehicle, or D plates in Wales. Learner drivers cannot drive on a motorway. If you drive a car, you must be with someone who is over 21 and who has had a full licence for over three years.2. Pass a written theory te st. Pass a practical driving test

جب آپ گاڑی یا موٹر سائیکل چلانا سیکھ رہے ہوتے ہیں تو آپ کو پروویژنل لائسنس کی ضرورت ہوتی ہے۔ آپ کو ایل پلیٹ لگانی ہوتی ہے یا ڈی پلیٹ اگر آپ ویلز میں ہیں۔ لرنرز ڈرائیور کو موٹروے پہ گاڑی نہیں چلانی چاہئے۔ اگر آپ گاڑی چلانا سیکھ رہے ہیں تو آپ کو سکھانے والے کی 21 سال کی عمر اور اس کے پاس تین سالہ ڈرائیونگ لائسنس ہونا چاہئے۔ اپنی تیوری پاس کریں اور اپنا ڈرائیونگ ٹیسٹ پاس کریں

Drivers may use their licence until they are 70. After that the licence is valid for three years at a time. In Northern Ireland, a newly-qualified driver must display an R-Plate (for registered driver) for one year

جب آپ کی عمر 70 سال سے اوپر ہو جائے تو ہر تین سال کے بعد لائسنس رینیو کرانا پڑتا ہے۔ ناردرن آئرلینڈ میں جب ڈرائیونگ پاس کریں تو ایک سال تک R پلیٹ لگانی پڑتی ہے۔

If you have a licence from a country outside the EU, you may use it in the UK for up to 12 months.

اگر آپ کے پاس EU کے علاوہ کسی اور ملک کا لائسنس ہے تو آپ ایک سال تک یو کے میں یوز کر سکتے ہیں۔

It is a criminal offence to have a car without proper motor insurance. Drivers without insurance can receive very high fines. It is also illegal to allow someone to use your car if they are not insured to drive it.

انشورنس کے بغیر گاڑی رکھنا جرم ہے اور بھاری جرمانہ ہو سکتا ہے۔ اور کسی کو گاڑی بغیر انشورنس کے دینا غیر قانونی ہے۔

*Inventory is a list of furniture or fittings in the property.
*YPBA is given to you if you are 16 or 17 and unemployed *People can drive a car at the age of 17.
*People pass their AGCSE at the age of 18

A tax to drive your car on the roads. This is called road tax. Your vehicle must have a road tax disc which shows you have paid. You can buy this at the post office. If you do not pay the road tax, your vehicle may be clamped or towed away. If your vehicle is over three years old, you must take it every year for a Ministry of Transport (MOT) test.

روڈز پر گاڑی چلانے کیلئے جو ٹیکس دیتے ہیں اسے روڈ ٹیکس کہتے ہیں اور ٹیکس ڈسک گاڑی پر لگائیں کہ آپ نے ٹیکس دیا ہے۔ آپ پوسٹ آفس سے خرید سکتے ہیں۔ اگر آپ ٹیکس نہ دیں تو آپ کی گاڑی کلمپ ہو جائیگی یا ضبط ہو جائیگی۔

If you do not have an MOT certificate, your insurance will not be valid.

اگر آپ کے پاس MOT نہ ہو تو آپ کی انشورنس نہیں ہو سکتی۔

Everyone in a vehicle should wear a seat belt. Children under 12 years of age may need a special booster seat. Motorcyclists and their passengers must wear a crash helmet (this law does not apply to Sikh men if they are wearing a turban). It is illegal to drive while holding a mobile phone.

ہر ایک کو گاڑی میں سیٹ بیلٹ باندھنی چاہئے 12 سال سے کم عمر بچے کو بوسٹر سیٹ پہننی چاہئے۔ موٹر سائیکل چلانے والے کو ہیلمٹ پہننا چاہئے (یہ قانون سکھوں پر لاگو نہیں ہوتا) موبائیل فون ہاتھ میں رکھ کر گاڑی چلانا غیر قانونی ہے

For cars and motorcycles the speed limits are: 30 miles per hour (mph) in built-up areas, unless a sign shows a different limit 60 mph on single carriageways 70 mph on motorways and dual carriageways Speed limits are lower for buses, lorries and cars pulling caravans.

گاڑی اور موٹر سائیکل چلانے کی سپیڈ لمٹ ہے 30 مایل رہائشی علاقے میں یا اگر کوئی سپیڈ لمٹ کا سائن ملے تو اس کے مطابق۔ 60 سنگل کیرج وے پہ اور 70 موٹر وے پہ جبکہ بس، لاری اور کاروان کھینچنے والی گاڑیوں کی سپیڈ کم ہوتی ہے۔

It is illegal to drive when you are over the alcohol limit or drunk. The police can stop you and give you a test to see how much alcohol you have in your body. This is called a breathalyser test. If a driver has more than the permitted amount of alcohol (called being 'over the limit') or refuses to take the test, he or she will be arrested.

شراب پی کر گاڑی چلانا غیر قانونی ہے۔ پولیس آپ کو روک کر چیک کر سکتی ہے کہ کتنی آپ نے پی رکھی ہے۔ اس آلے کو بریتھالائزر ٹیسٹ کہتے ہیں اگر ڈرائیور نے زیادہ پی رکھی ہو تو اسے اوور دا لمٹ کہتے ہیں

Chapter 5 Everyday Needs

67

Chapter 5

People who drink and drive can expect to be disqualified from driving for a long period.

جو لوگ پی کر گاڑی چلاتے ہیں انہیں لمبے عرصے تک ڈسکوالیفائیڈ کر دیا جاتا ہے۔

If you are involved in accidnet

اگر آپ کسی حادثے میں ملوث ہوتے ہیں تو بھاگیں مت یہ جرم ہے

☐ Don't drive away without stopping - this is a criminal offence

☐ Call the police and ambulance on 999 or 112 if someone is injured

☐ Get the names, addresses, vehicle registration numbers and insurance details of the other drivers contact your insurance company as soon as possible

نام، پتہ اور گاڑی کا رجسٹر نمبر اور انشورنس حاصل کریں اور جتنی جلدی ہو سکے اپنی انشورنس کمپنی کو فون کریں

At present, UK citizens do not have to carry identity (ID) cards documents as proof of identity.

یوکے کے لوگ ID اپنے پاس نہیں رکھتے

☐ Official documents from the Home Office showing your immigration status

ہوم آفس کے پیپر جس میں آپ کا ویزا اسٹیٹس ہو

☐ A certificate of identity

☐ A passport or travel document

☐ A National Insurance (NI) number card

☐ A provisional or full driving licence

☐ A recent gas, electricity or phone bill showing your name and addre

68

Chapter 5 Practice Exam

(1) The seller sets a price for the house and buyers make offers over that amount. This describes the purchasing process in
A. England
B. Scotland
C. The United Kingdom
D. Northern Ireland

(2) Who runs shared ownership schemes?
A. Landlords
B. Tenants
C. Housing associations
D. Local authorities

(3) While looking for accommodation, you may be discriminated because of race
A. If the landlord or a landlord's close relative is sharing the accommodation
B. If the accommodation is in an upscale area
C. If the landlord is of the same race as you
D. No, never

(4) If you are setting up home after being released from prison,
A. You are not eligible for any help from the government
B. You may be entitled to a Community Care Grant
C. You are not eligible for Council Housing
D. You may be entitled to a Social Fund

(5) You can get advice about changing your providers, from:
A. Transco for gas, Energy watch for electricity, Ofcom for telephone
B. Ofcom for gas, Energy watch for electricity, Transco for telephone
C. Transco for all providers
D. Ofcom for telephone and Energy watch for gas and electricity

(6) The amount of Council Tax you pay depends on
A. the size and value of your house or flat
B. the size of your house or flat
C. the value of your house or flat
D. your income

(7) Euro will only replace the Pound Sterling if
A. the UK joins the European Union
B. the UK government decides so
C. the British people agree with it in a referendum
D. the Queen removes her veto

(8) When banks decide whether or not to give you credit, they consider
A. your address, gender, race
B. your age, gender and credit record
C. your occupation and age
D. your occupation, address, salary and previous credit record

(9) You don't have to pay for your prescriptions if you are
A. on paternity leave
B. 18 years old and working in Scotland
C. unemployed and receiving Jobseeker's Allowance
D. self-employed and contributing to National Insurance

(10) Free dental treatment is available to you if you are
A. a self-employed single mother with a 3 years old child
B. 65 years old and live in Scotland
C. 19 years old and studying in England
D. unemployed and receiving Jobseeker's Allowance

(11) Health visitor is
A. any person who comes to a Primary Health Care Centre
B. a Patient Advice and Liaison Service (PALS) employee
C. a pregnant woman or a woman with a baby under 12 months old
D. a qualified nurse who can advise you about caring for your baby

*provisional license while you are learning to drive *With this you are allowed to drive a motorcycle up to 125cc or a car *If you drive a car, you must be with someone who is over 21 and who has had a full license for over three years *You must put L plates on the vehicle, or D plates in Wales

Chapter 5

(12) A newborn must be registered within
A. two weeks of the birth B. the same day when he or she was born
C. six weeks of the birth D. six months of the birth

(13) Integrated Schools are
A. Some schools in Northern Ireland that aim to bring children of different religions together
B. Faith schools
C. Schools that are not run or paid for by the state
D. Schools where both boys and girls learn together and are usually close to a child's home

(14) EMA is
A. a grant for students from families with low incomes with their university tuition
B. an allowance to pay for school meals for low income families
C. an endowment, in Scotland only
D. an allowance for 16-year-olds from low income families

(15) You can apply for a free TV licence if
A. you are blind
B. rent a room in a house that has a licence
C. you are under 18
D. you are over 75

(16) National Trust is
A. a foundation that helps students from low income families
B. a charity that offers help to pet owners who cannot afford a vet
C. the organisation that protects parts of the countryside and places of interest in the UK
D. the name of Scottish single curriculum

(17) If you have a provisional driving licence in Wales, you have to display a
A. D plate   B. L plate
C. R plate   D. N plate

(18) You car may be towed away if
A. you do not pay the road tax   B. you drive without insurance
C. you drive without an MOT certificate   D. you drive without your seatbelt on

(19) In Scotland, eye tests are free for
A. Children, people with certain eye conditions and people receiving certain benefits
B. People over 60 and children   C. Everyone
D. People on Jobseekers Allowance, children and people over 60

(20) Advice on contraception is available from
A. the National Childbirth Trust   B. Citizens Advice Bureau
C. the Family Planning Association (FPA) D. CRB or Disclosure Scotland

(21) Discrimination laws do not apply if you
A. Are in performing, modelling, sport and agriculture
B. Are working for someone in their own home
C. Are working with children or vulnerable people
D. Lied about your qualifications

(22) Mortgage is
A. A special loan from a bank or a building society, used to pay for a home
B. A check on the house done by a surveyor
C. The name of the deposit left to the owner at the beginning of tenancy
D. The name of a real estate purchase agreement in Scotland

(23) You are more likely to obtain council housing if you
A. Are self-employed   B. Are unemployed
C. Have a local connection D. Are homeless, have children or chronic ill health

*Discount tickets are available for families, people aged 60 and over, disabled people, students and people under 26
*18 to drive a medium sized lorry, and 21 to drive a large lorry or bus.

(24) Lease is
A. The benefit available to homeless
B. An ownership scheme ran by Housing Associations
C. The list of furniture or fittings in the property
D. The document that you sign when you rent a house or flat

(25) The money that you give your landlord at the beginning of your tenancy, to cover the cost of potential damage, is called
A. Inventory, and usually equals 1 month's rent
B. Lease, and usually equals 3 months' rent
C. Deposit, and usually equals 1 month's rent
D. Mortgage, and usually equals 2 months' rent

(26) You may not raise your tenant's rent without his or her agreement
A. False   C. True, unless all the prices have gone up in the country
B. True   D. False, it can be raised with two weeks notice

(27) If you are homeless, the local authority may offer you a place to live, if you
A. Prove that you haven't made yourself intentionally homeless
B. Have been homeless for more than 6 months
C. Don't have a connection with the area
D. Prove that there is nobody else who can help you

(28) If you pay your water rates in one payment, it is called
A. Installment B. Domestic rate
C. Lump sum D. Bill

(29) In the UK , the electricity is supplied at
A. 220 volts   B. 120 volts
C. 140 volts   D. 240 volts

(30) If your phone has been disconnected because you failed to pay a bill,
A. you may never be able to obtain a phone line again
B. you can call Transco and contract a different provider
C. you will have to pay another charge to get it reconnected
D. you will be reconnected automatically as soon as you pay the outstanding bill

(31) To get rid of an old fridge, bed or wardrobe, you have to
A. place these items into bins with wheels
B. contact your local authority to arrange this
C. cover these items in plastic
D. place these items outside

(32) Your home must be insured against fire, theft and accidental damage
A. if you buy it with a mortgage   B. always
C. only if you are a tenant   D. whenever you wish

(33) Bad neighbours can be evicted from their homes
A. if all the neighbours agree   B. by a court's decision
C. by the local authority D. by their landlord, and if they own their home, by the police

(34) The way many people fall into debt is by
A. using debit cards and cash cards
B. using bank accounts and building society accounts
C. becoming members of Credit Unions
D. using credit cards and store cards

(35) If you don't have enough money to live on,
A. you can apply for a loan from your Credit Union
B. you can get a mortgage from a local bank
C. you may apply for benefits available through the social security system
D. you may not have a bank account

*If you have a license from a country outside the EU, you may use it in the UK for up to 12 months. Children under 12 years of age may need a special booster seat

Chapter 5

(36) Who is entitled to apply for council accommodations?
A. Only people with priority needs
B. Everyone
C. Only people who paid enough Council Tax
D. Only people who receive Social Security benefits

(37) Insurance is compulsory if
A. you have a car or motorcycle
B. you travel abroad
C. you have a mobile phone
D. you need medical treatment abroad

(38) When should you look for a GP?
A. As soon as you move to a new area.
B. As soon as you get ill
C. As soon as you have a medical emergency
D. Once you receive a medical card

(39) If you need to see a specialist,
A. You have to contact that specialist directly
B. You have to go to your GP first.
C. You can find a specialist in any hospital
D. You can find a specialist in any Primary Health Care Centre.

(40) School uniforms and sports wear
A. is paid by the schools
B. must be paid by the parents
C. is paid by the Citizens Advice Bureau if you are on low incomes
D. is distributed free of charge in schools

(41) Parents in Scotland may withdraw their children from
A. RE: Religious Education
B. FE: Further Education
C. PE: Physical Education
D. A home-schooling agreement

(42) Key Stage tests are also called
A. GCSEs
B. SATs
C. EMAs
D. A levels

(43) A home-schooling agreement is
A. a contract whereby a child is educated at home, by private teachers, and not in school
B. the contract whereby a Scottish student repays his or her tuition fees after graduating
C. a list of things that both the school and the parent agree to do to ensure agood education for the child
D. a report on child's progress in the school

(44) What is the fastest you are allowed to drive in the United Kingdom?
A. 70 mph
B. 60 mph
C. 80 mph
D. 75 mph

(45) The department that you will probably attend if you need minor tests at a hospital, is called
A. Patient Advice and Liaison
B. Outpatients
C. A&E
D. NHS

(46) If you are going to stay overnight in a hospital, you should take with you
A. night clothes and food
B. towel, bedsheets, toothbrush
C. nothing. Everything is provided
D. towel, night clothes, things for washing, dressing gown

(47) Your medical card
A. is given to you by your GP
B. can be applied for at any pharmacy
C. tracks your NI contributions, which pay for the NHS
D. is sent to you by your local health authority

*Drivers may use their license until they are 70. After that the license is valid for three years at a time.
*In Northern Ireland, a newly-qualified driver must display an R-Plate (for registered driver) for one year after passing the test.

(48) Public schools are
A. All state-owned schools
B. Independent secondary schools
C. All schools that are not linked to the Church of England or the Roman Catholic Church
D. Schools where Skills for Life courses are available

(49) To buy a lottery ticket or a scratch card, you must be at least
A. 16 years old   B. 18 years old
C. 14 years old   D. 21 years old

(50) A deposit paid to the landlord at the beginning of a tenancy is ot|iinl to one month's rent.
Is this statement true or false?
A True   B False

(51) What does the film classification PG mean?
A Children under 15 are not allowed to see or rent the film
B No one under 18 is allowed to see or rent the film
C Suitable for anyone aged four years or over
D Suitable for everyone but some parts of the film might be unsuitable for children

(52) Interest rates in credit unions are usually higher than banks.
Is this statement true or false?
A True   B False

(53) Select the correct statement
A Children are allowed to work for the full duration of their school holidays B Children must have at least two consecutive weeks a year during their holidays where they do not work

(54) If you cannot find a GP, who can you ask for help to find one?
A Citizens Advice Bureau B The local health authority C The local hospital D Your local MP

(55) If a child does not attend school, that child's parent or guardian
may be prosecuted. Is this statement true or false?
A True B False

(56) What are courses for people who want to improve their English language skills called?
A EAL   B EEE   C ESOL   D NHS16

(57) What denomination of bank notes do not exist in the UK?
A £5   B £20   C £50   D £100

(58) People under 18 cannot drink alcohol in a pub but they can buy it In
a supermarket or an off-licence. Is this statement true or false?
A True B False

(59) A tenancy agreement will be for a fixed period of time. Is this statement true or false?
A True B False

(60) Bank notes from Scotland and Northern Ireland are not valid
in the rest of the UK. Is this statement true or false?
A True B False

(61) Insurance for a car or motorcycle is optional. Is this statement true or false?
A True   B False

(62) At what voltage is electricity supplied in the UK?
A 1000 volts B 110 volts C 240 volts D 50 volts

(63) When are you likely to be required to prove your identity?
Select two options from below
A When opening a bank account   B When applying for Housing Benefit
C When purchasing National Rail tickets D When travelling between England and Wales

Chapter 5

(64) In primary schools boys and girls usually learn together. Is this statement true or false?
  A True   B False

(65) What is the purpose of Housing Benefit?
  A To help you buy a home   B To help you fix a home
  C To help you pay your rent   D To help you sell a home

(66) People in the UK who buy their own home usually pay for it with a mortgage. Is this statement true or false?
  A True   B False

(67) A tenant must leave a home if the landlord has a court order requiring the tenant to do so. Is this statement true or false?
  A True   B False

(68) When will the British government adopt the euro as the UK's
  A 2010   B 2015
  C Never   D When the British people vote for it in a referendum

(69) Somebody aged 16 can drink wine or beer with a meal in a hotel or restaurant. Is this statement true or false?
  A True   B False

(70) If you have a driving licence from a country outside the EU, yt< use it in the UK for up to 12 months. Is this statement trut ff <
  A True B False

(72) How can you compare qualifications from another country with those in the UK?
  A By asking your neighbour   B By contacting the National Academic Recognition Infill"
  C By visiting your local library D By writing to potential employers

(73) Who should you approach to get information about local secondary schools?
  A NHS Direct   B The local education authority
  C Your local MP   D Your nearest school

(74) Which of the following statements is correct?
  A If you need to see a specialist for medical treatment then you must see your GP first
  B You should always go directly to a specialist if you believe you know the medical treatment you require

1 B	2 C	3 A	4 A	5 A	6 A	7 C	8 D	9 C	10 D
C	11 D	12 C	13 A	14 D	15 D	16 C	17 A	18 A	19 C
	20 C	21 B	22 A	23 D	24 D	25 C	26 B	27 A	28 A
	29 A	30 C	31 B	32 A	33 B	34 D	35 C	36 B	37 C
	38 A	39 B	40 B	41 A	42 B	43 C	44 A	45 B	46 C
	47 B	48 B	49 A	50 D	51 B	52 B	53 A	54 A	55 C
	56 D	57 B	58A	59 B	60 B	61 C	62 A	63 A	64 C
	65 A	66 A	67 D	68 A	69A	70 B	71B	72 A	73 B
74 A									

30 miles per hour (mph) in built-up areas, unless a sign shows a different limit 60 mph on single carriageways. 70 mph on motorways and dual carriageways, speed limits are lower for buses, lorries and cars pulling caravans.

74

Employments روزگار

The home office provides guidance on who is allowed to work in the UK.

ہوم آفس معلومات دیتا ہے کہ یو کے میں کون کام کر سکتا ہے اور کون نہیں۔

Not every one in the UK is allowed to work and some people need work permits, so it is important to check your status before taking up work.

اگر کوئی یو کے میں ہے تو اس کا مطلب یہ نہیں کہ وہ کام بھی کر سکتا ہے کام کرنے سے پہلے اپنا ویزا اسٹیٹس دیکھنا پڑتا ہے اور کچھ لوگوں کو کام کرنے کیلئے ورک پرمٹ چاہئے ہوتا ہے۔

Also employers have to check that anyone they employ is legally entitled to work in UK.

اور جو آپ کو جاب دیتا ہے وہ بھی چیک کرے کہ آپ قانونی طور پہ کام کر بھی سکتے ہیں یا نہیں۔

Jobs are usually advertised in local and national news papers, at the local job centre and in employment agencies.

جاب کا اشتہار عام طور پہ لوکل اور نیشنل اخبار میں آتا ہے یا لوکل جاب سینٹر میں یا ایجنسی میں

Some jobs are advertised on supermarket notice boards and in shop windows. These jobs are usually part-time and the wages are often quite low.

کچھ جاب سپر مارکیٹ کے نوٹس بورڈ پر یا کھڑکی پہ لگی ہوتی ہیں یہ جاب عام طور پر پارٹ ٹائم ہوتی ہیں اور سیلری کم ہوتی ہے۔

Jobcentre Plus is run by a government department - the Department for Work and Pensions.

جاب سینٹر گورنمنٹ کا ڈیپارٹمنٹ چلاتا ہے جسے ڈیپارٹمنٹ فار ورک اور پینشن کہتے ہیں۔

If you have qualifications from another country, you can find out how they compare with qualifications in the UK at the National Academic Recognition Information Centre (NARIC)

اگر آپ کی تعلیم کسی اور ملک کی ہے تو آپ اسے انگلینڈ سے کمپیر کر سکتے ہیں اور مزید معلومات NARIC سے لے سکتے ہیں۔

When you are applying for a job during the interview, it is important to be honest about your qualifications and experience.

جب آپ جاب اپلائی کرتے ہیں تو انٹرویو کے دوران اپنی تعلیم اور تجربے کے بارے میں سچ بتائیں

If an employer later finds out that you gave incorrect information, you might lose your job.

اگر جاب دینے والے کو بعد میں پتہ چل جائے کہ آپ نے غلط بیانی سے کام لیا ہے تو ہو سکتا ہے آپ کو نوکری سے ہاتھ دھونے پڑیں۔

*Key Points to Remember in Chapter 6

*People who are self employed need to pay NI contributions themselves: Class 2 contributions. Class 4 contributions are paid alongside their income tax.

Chapter 6 Employments

75

Chapter 6

For many jobs you need to fill in an application form or send a copy of your curriculum vitae (CV) with a covering letter or letter of application.

زیادہ تر نوکریوں کیلئے آپ کو ایپلیکیشن فارم دینا پڑتا ہے یا سی وی کی کاپی کورنگ لیٹر یا ایپلیکیشن لیٹر کے ساتھ بھیجنی پڑتی ہے

A covering letter is usually a short letter attached to a completed application form, while a letter of application gives more detailed information on why you are applying for the job and why you think you are suitable.

کورنگ لیٹر ایک شارٹ لیٹر ہوتا ہے جو ایپلیکیشن فارم کے ساتھ لگایا جاتا ہے جبکہ ایپلیکیشن لیٹر میں یہ تفصیل ہوتی ہے کہ کیوں آپ جاب اپلائی کر رہے ہیں اور کیوں آپ سوٹ ایبل ہیں

Your CV gives specific details on your education, qualifications, previous employment skills and interests.

آپ کی سی وی آپ کی تعلیم، کوالیفیکیشن، اور پہلی جاب اور کیا مہارت اور دلچسپی رکھتے ہیں کے بارے میں تفصیل سے بتاتی ہے

It is important to type any letters and your CV on a computer or word processor as this improves your chance of being called for an interview.

یہ ضروری ہے کہ ایپلیکیشن اور سی وی کمپیوٹر پر ٹائپ کریں اس طرح سے آپ کے انٹرویو پر بلانے کے زیادہ چانس ہوتے ہیں

Employers often ask for the names and addresses of one or two referees. These are people such as your current or previous employer or college tutor. Personal friends or members of your family are not normally acceptable as referees.

ایمپلائر اکثر ریفرینس کا پوچھتے ہیں آپ کا پرانا ایمپلائر یا کالج ٹیوٹر آپ کے ریفرنس بن سکتے ہیں فیملی ممبر آپ کا ریفرنس نہیں دے سکتے۔

In job descriptions and interviews, employers should give full details of what the job involves, including the pay, holidays and working conditions.

جاب کے بارے میں ایمپلائر کو سب کچھ بتانا چاہئے جیسے کہ جاب میں کیا کیا کرنا ہے تنخواہ کتنی ہے چھٹیاں کتنی ہیں وغیرہ۔

Asking some questions in the interview shows you are interested and can improve your chance of getting the job.

انٹرویو کے دوران سوالات پوچھنا ظاہر کرتا ہے کہ آپ کو جاب میں دلچسپی ہے اور چانسز بڑھ جاتے ہیں

For some jobs, particularly if the work involves working with children or vulnerable people, the employer will ask for your permission to do a criminal record check.. Get more information from the Home Office Criminal Records Bureau

کچھ جابز کیلئے جیسے کہ ناتجھ افراد کے ساتھ کام کرنے کیلئے ہوسکتا ہے ایمپلائر آپ سے کہے کہ CRB کرائیں۔ آپ اس کے بارے میں معلومات ہوم آفس سے لے سکتے ہیں

For workers aged 22 and above £5.35 an hour
* for 18-21 year olds - £4.45 an hour.
* for 16-17 year olds - £3.30 an hour.

Learn direct offers a range of online training courses at centres across the country.

لرن ڈائریکٹ پورے ملک میں آن لائن ٹریننگ کورسز کرواتا ہے

Some people do voluntary work and this can be a good way to support your local community and organisations which depend on volunteers. It also provides useful experience that can help with future job applications.

کچھ لوگ والینٹری ورک کرتے ہیں اور اس طرح لوکل کمیونٹی کو اور اداروں کو فائدہ ہوتا ہے اور والینٹیر کو بھی تجربہ ہوتا ہے اور جاب حاصل کرنے میں آسانی ہوتی ہے

It is against the law for employers to discriminate against someone at work.

یہ قانون کے خلاف ہے کہ امپلائر کسی کو کمتر سمجھ کہ جاب نہ دے۔

A person should not be refused work, training or promotion or treated unfavourably because of their sex nationality, race, colour or ethnic group, disability or religion.

کسی کو بھی نیشنیلٹی، ریس، کلر، یا اقلیتی یا معذوری یا اسے مذہبی سمجھ کر جاب یا ٹریننگ دینے سے انکار نہیں کرنا چاہئے

In Northern Ireland, the law also bans discrimination on grounds of religious belief or political opinion.

ناردرن آئرلینڈ میں قانونی جرم ہے کہ مذہب اور سیاست کی وجہ سے امتیازی سلوک نہیں کرنا چاہئے

Discrimination is not against the law when the job involves working for someone in their own home.

کسی کے گھر میں کام کرنے سے یہ قانون نہیں لگتا۔

You can get more information about the law and racial discrimination from the Commission for Racial Equality.

نسلی امتیاز کے بارے میں ریشیل کمیشن فار ایکوالٹی ڈیل کرتا ہے

The Equal Opportunities Commission can help with sex discrimination issues

برابری کے حقوق ایکول اوپرچیونٹی ڈیل کرتا ہے

Disability Rights Commission deals with disability issues

معذوری کے حقوق ڈس ایبلٹی کمیشن ڈیل کرتا ہے

Men and women can be victims of sexual harassment at work. If this happens to you, tell a friend, colleague or trade union representative and ask the person harassing you to stop.

مرد اور عورت جسمانی بے حرمتی کا شکار ہو سکتے ہیں۔ اگر ایسا ہوتا ہے تو کسی دوست سے بات کریں یا ٹریڈ یونین سے بات کریں جو آپ کو ہراساں کر رہا ہے

*Adults who have been unemployed for 18 months are usually required to join New Deal if they wish to continue receiving benefit *Women are entitled to at least 26 weeks' maternity leave *Men are entitled to have 2 weeks paternity leave if have been working with the company for more than 26 weeks.

77

Chapter 6

Both employers and employees have legal responsibilities at work. Employers have to pay employees for the work that they do, treat them fairly and take responsible care for their health and safety.

امپلائر اور ورکر دونوں کام پر ذمہ دار افراد ہوتے ہیں امپلائر ورکر کو کام کرنے کے پیسے دیتا ہے اور ان کی سیفٹی کا اور صحت کا خیال رکھتا ہے

Within two months of starting a new job, your employer should give you a written contract or statement with all the details and conditions for your work. This should include your responsibilities, pay, working hours, holidays, sick pay and pension.

نئی جاب شروع ہونے کے دو ماہ بعد آپ کے امپلائر کو کنٹریکٹ سائن کرانا چاہئے جس میں کام کی تمام شرائط ہوں۔ جیسے کہ آپ کی کیا ذمہ داری ہے تنخواہ، چھٹیاں، پینشن وغیرہ

It should also include the period of notice that both you and your employer should give for the employment to end.

اس میں جاب چھوڑنے کی مدت کا نوٹس کب دینا ہے یہ بھی شامل ہوتا ہے

The contract or written statement is an important document and is very useful if there is ever a disagreement about your work, pay or conditions.

کنٹریکٹ ایک اہم دستاویز ہے اگر کوئی مسئلہ ہو تو دستاویز میں چیک کیا جا سکتا ہے

The compulsory school leaving age is 16.

سولہ سال کی عمر میں بچے سکول سے خارج ہو جاتا ہے

From October 2006 the rates are as follows:
for workers aged 22 and above £5.35 an hour
for 18-21 year olds - £4.45 an hour
for 16-17 year olds - £3.30 an hour

Employers who pay their workers less than this are breaking the law.

امپلائر جو کم تنخواہ دیتے ہیں وہ قانون کی خلاف ورزی کرتے ہیں

Your contract or statement will show number of hours you are expected to work.

آپ کے کنٹریکٹ میں یہ لکھا ہوتا ہے کہ کتنے گھنٹے آپ کام کر سکتے ہیں

Your employer might ask you if you can work more hours than this and it is your decision whether or not you do.

ہو سکتا ہے آپ کا امپلائر آپ سے زیادہ کام کرنے کو کہے اور یہ آپ کی مرضی ہے کہ آپ کریں یا نہ کریں

Your employer cannot require you to work more hours than the hours agreed on your contract.

آپ کا امپلائر آپ سے کنٹریکٹ آورز سے زیادہ کام کرنے کو نہیں کہہ سکتا۔

*The State Pension age for men is currently 65 years of age and for women it is 60, but the State Pension age for women will increase to 65 in stages between 2010 and 2020 Young people who have been unemployed for 6 months sign new deal.

If you need to be absent from work, for example if you are ill or you have a medical appointment it is important to tell your employer as soon as you can in advance.

اگر آپ نے کام سے چھٹی کرنی ہے یا بیمار ہیں تو جتنی جلدی ہو سکے امپلائر کو بتائیں

Most employees who are 16 or over are entitled to at least four weeks, paid holiday every year. This includes time for national holidays

سولہ سال کی عمر سے زیادہ عمر کے ورکر کو چار ہفتے کی تنخواہ سمیت چھٹی ملتی ہے

Your employer must give you a pay slip, or a similar written statement each time you are paid.

آپ کے امپلائر کو پے سلپ دینی چاہیے ہر مرتبہ جب وہ آپ کو پیسے دیتا ہے

This must show exactly how much money has been taken off for tax and national insurance contributions.

اس میں یہ لکھا ہونا چاہیے کہ نیشنل انشورنس اور ٹیکس کے کتنے پیسے کٹے ہیں

For most people, taxes are automatically taken from their earnings by the employer and paid directly to HM Revenue and Customs, the government department responsible for collecting taxes.

زیادہ تر لوگوں کے ٹیکس خود بخود کٹ جاتے ہیں اور ایچ ایم ریونیو کو چلے جاتے ہیں یہ گورنمنٹ ڈیپارٹمنٹ ہے جو ٹیکس اکٹھا کرتا ہے

If you are self-employed, you need to pay your own tax.

اگر آپ سیلف امپلائیڈ ہیں تو آپ کو اپنا ٹیکس خود دینا ہوتا ہے

Money raised from income tax pays for government services such as roads, education, police and the armed forces.

جو اِنکم ٹیکس سے پیسہ آتا ہے وہ سڑکیں بنانے، تعلیم، پولیس اور آرمی میں خرچ ہوتا ہے۔

If you receive one, it is important to complete it and return the form as soon as possible.

اگر آپ کو ٹیکس فارم ملے تو فل کر کے جتنی جلدی ہو سکے واپس بھیجیں۔

Almost everybody in the UK who is in paid work, including self-employed have to pay NI contributions.

ہر ایک جو کام کرتا ہے اسے نیشنل انشورنس دینا ہوتا ہے

Money raised from NI contributions is used to pay contributory benefits such as the State Retirement Pension and helps fund the National Health Service.

نیشنل انشورنس کا پیسہ بینیفٹس جیسے پینشن اور نیشنل ہیلتھ سروس میں خرچ ہوتا ہے

Chapter 6

Employees have their NI contributions deducted from their pay by their employer every week or month.

نیشنل انشورینس ہر ہفتے یا ہر مہینے آپ کی تنخواہ سے کٹتا ہے

People who are self employed need to pay NI contributions themselves are Class 2 contributions, Class 4 contributions are on the profits from their trade trade or business.

جو سیلف ایمپلائیڈ ہیں وہ کلاس 2 انشورینس دیتے ہیں اور جو بزنس کرنے والے کلاس 4 انشورینس دیتے ہیں

Anyone who does not pay enough NI contributions will not be able to receive certain benefits, such as Jobseekers Allowance or Maternity Pay, and may not receive a full state retirement pension.

جو انشورینس نہیں دیتے ان کو جاب سیکر الاؤنس میٹرنٹی پے پنشن یا اور قسم کے بینیفٹ نہیں ملتے۔

Just before their 16th birthday, all young people in the UK are sent a National Insurance number.

16 سال کی عمر کے جب ہونے والے ہوتے ہیں تو آپ کو نیشنل انشورینس دیا جاتا ہے

This is a unique number for each person and it tracks their National Insurance contributions.

یہ ایک خاص نمبر ہے جس سے آپ نے کتنی انشورینس دی ہے پتہ چل جاتا ہے

You need a National Insurance number when you start work.

آپ کو نیشنل انشورینس نمبر چاہئے ہوتا ہے جب آپ کام شروع کرتے ہیں

If you do not have a National Insurance number, you can apply for one through Jobcentre Plus or your local Social Security Office.

اگر آپ کے پاس نیشنل انشورینس نہیں ہے تو آپ جاب سینٹر یا لوکل سوشل سکیورٹی آفس سے لے سکتے ہیں

Everyone in the UK who has paid enough National Insurance contributions will get a State Pension when they retire.

ہر ایک جس نے نیشنل انشورینس دیا ہے ریٹائر ہونے پر پنشن ملے گی۔

The State Pension age for men is currently 65 years of age and for women it is 60, but the State Pension age for women will increase to 65 in stages between 2010 and 2020.

پنشن کی عمر اس وقت مردوں کیلئے 65 اور عورتوں کیلئے 60 سال ہے 2010 اور 2020 تک ایک جیسی ہو جائے گی۔

In addition to a State Pension, many people also receive a pension through their work and some also pay into a personal pension plan too.

گورنمنٹ کی پنشن کے علاوہ کام کی جگہ سے بھی پنشن ملتی ہے اور کچھ لوگ ذاتی پنشن پلان بھی خریدتے ہیں

Employers have a legal duty to make sure the workplace is safe. If you are worried about health and safety at your workplace, talk to your supervisor, manager or trade union representative.

املایئر کی ذمہ داری ہوتی ہے کہ کام کی جگہ کو سیف رکھے اور اگر آپ کو فکر ہے کہ جگہ سیف نہیں ہے تو آپ مینیجر کو یا یونین کو کمپلین کر سکتے ہیں

Trade unions are organisations that aim to improve the pay and working conditions of their members. They also give their members advice and support on problems at work.

ٹریڈ یونین کام کرنے والوں کی بہتری کیلئے کام کرتی ہیں جیسے کہ تنخواہ یا کام کی جگہ بہتر بنانا۔ اور مشورے دینا اور سپورٹ کرنا ہے

If you have problems of any kind at work, speak to your supervisor manager, trade union representative

اگر کام پر آپ کو کوئی مسئلہ ہے تو اپنے مینیجر سے بات کریں، سپروائزر یا ٹریڈ یونین سے بات کریں۔

An employee can be dismissed immediately for serious misconduct at work.

ملازم کو کسی بھی وقت سنگین بد اخلاقی کی وجہ سے نکالا جا سکتا ہے

Anyone who cannot do their job properly, or is unacceptably late or absent from work, should be given a warning by their employer. If their work, punctuality or attendance does not improve, the employer can give them notice to leave job.

جو کوئی صحیح کام نہ کرے یا وقت پر کام پر نہ آئے اسے پہلے وارننگ دینی چاہیے۔ اگر پھر بھی وہ وقت پر نہ آئے تو املائر اسے جاب چھوڑنے کا نوٹس دے دے۔

It is against the law for employers to dismiss someone from work unfairly.

کسی کو بلا وجہ جاب سے نکالنا غیر قانونی ہے

If this happens to you, or life at work is made so difficult that you feel you have to leave, you may be able to get compensation if you take your case to an Employment Tribunal.

اگر آپ کے ساتھ ایسا ہوتا ہے یا کام پر حالات اتنے خراب ہو جائیں کہ آپ کو جاب چھوڑنی پڑے تو آپ کمپینسیشن کلیم کر سکتے ہیں اگر آپ اپنا کیس املائمنٹ ٹرائبیونل کے پاس لے جائیں۔

This is a court which specialises in employment matters. You normally only have three months to make a complaint.

یہ کورٹ روزگار کے مسائل حل کرتا ہے اور آپ کو جاب چھوڑنے کے تین مہینے کے اندر شکایت کرنی ہوتی ہے

Chapter 6 Employments

81

Chapter 6

If you lose your job because the company you work for no longer needs someone to do your job, or cannot afford to employ you, you may be entitled to redundancy pay.

اگر آپ کی نوکری ختم ہو جاتی ہے اس لئے کہ جہاں آپ کام کرتے ہیں ان کو آپ کی ضرورت نہیں یا آپ کو تنخواہ نہیں دے سکتے تو آپ کو ریڈینسی پے مل سکتی ہے

Most people who become unemployed can claim Jobseeker's Allowance (JSA). This is currently available for men aged 18-65 and women aged 18-60

60-18 عمر کی خواتین اور 65-18 عمر کے مرد جو بے روزگار ہو جاتے ہیں وہ جاب سیکرالاؤنس کلیم کر سکتے ہیں

Unemployed 16 and 17-olds may not be eligible for Jobseeker's Allowance but may be able to claim a Young Person's Bridging Allowance (YPBA) instead.

سولہ اور سترہ سال کی عمر میں جاب سیکر تو نہیں ملتا مگر ان کو YPBA ملتا ہے

New Deal is a government programme that aims to give unemployed people help & support they need to get into work.

نیو ڈیل گورنمنٹ پروگرام ہے جو بے روزگار لوگوں کو کام حاصل کرنے میں مدد دیتا ہے

Young people who have been unemployed for 6 months and adults who have been unemployed for 18 months are usually required to join New Deal if they wish to continue receiving benefit.

جوان بچے 6 ماہ کے بعد سائن کرتے ہیں اور بالغ 18 مہینے کے بعد سائن کرتے ہیں

As soon as you become self-employed you should register yourself for tax and National Insurance by ringing the HM Revenue and Customs.

جوں ہی آپ سیلف امپلائیڈ ہوتے ہیں آپ ایچ ایم ریونیو کو فون کر کے ٹیکس اور نیشنل انشورینس رجسٹر کروائیں۔

Banks can give information and advice on setting up your own business and offer start-up loans

بینک آپ کو بزنس شروع کرنے کے بارے میں مشورے اور معلومات دیتا ہے

British citizens can work in any country that is a member of the European Economic Area (EEA).

برٹش سٹیزن کسی بھی یورپین یونین ملک میں کام کر سکتے ہیں

In general, they have the same employment rights as a citizen of that country or state.

82

Chapter 6 Employments

اور ان کو وہی حقوق حاصل ہیں جو اس ملک کے شہری کو حاصل ہیں

Women who are expecting a baby have a legal right to time off work for antenatal care.

خواتین جو پریگنینٹ ہیں قانونی طور پہ کام سے چھٹی لے سکتی ہیں

They are also entitled to at least 26 weeks' maternity leave. These rights apply to full-time and part-time workers and it makes no difference how long the woman has worked for her employer.

ان کو 26 ہفتوں کی ودیے چھٹی ہوتی ہے اس سے کوئی فرق نہیں پڑتا کہ اس کی جاب پارٹ ٹائم ہے یا فل ٹائم اور اس سے بھی کوئی فرق نہیں پڑتا کہ اس نے جاب کب شروع کی ہے۔

Fathers who have worked for their employer for at least 26 weeks are entitled to paternity leave, which provides up to two weeks' time off from work

پیٹرنٹی چھٹی جو کہ فادر کو ملتی ہے اگر اس نے کم از کم 26 ہفتے سے زیادہ عرصہ ہو گیا ہے کام کرتے ہوئے تو اسے 2 ہفتے کی ودیے تنخواہ ملے گی۔

The earliest legal age for children to do paid work is set at 14.

14 سال کی عمر میں قانونی طور پر آپ کام کر سکتے ہیں

There are a few exceptions that allow children under the age of 14 to work legally and these include specific work in performing, modelling, sport and agriculture. In order to do it. it is necessary to get a licence from the local authority.

14 سال سے کم عمر کے لوگ اس صورت میں کام کر سکتے ہیں کہ وہ ماڈلنگ، سپورٹس اور کھیتوں میں کام کریں اور اس کیلئے لوکل اتھارٹی سے لائسنس لیں

By law, children aged 14 to 16 can only do light work. There are particular jobs they are not allowed to do and these include delivering milk, selling alcohol, cigarettes or medicines, working in a kitchen or a chip shop, working with dangerous machinery

قانونی طور پر چودہ اور سولہ سال کے عمر کی کے لوگ ہلکا پھلکا کام کر سکتے ہیں۔ اور بھاری بھرکم کام جیسے گھروں میں دودھ ڈیلیور کرنا اور سیگریٹ بیچنا اور الکوحل اور دوائیاں وغیرہ کا کام نہیں کر سکتے۔

Children who work have to get an employment card from their local authority and a medical certificate for work.

جو بچے کام کرتے ہیں ان کو ایمپلائمنٹ کارڈ لینا پڑتا ہے اور میڈیکل کروانا ہوتا ہے کہ وہ کام کیلئے فٹ ہیں۔

Every child must have at least two consecutive weeks a year during the school holidays when they do not work

ہر بچے کو سال میں سکول سے چھٹیوں کے دوران ان دو ہفتے چھٹیاں کرنی چاہیں

83

Chapter 6

They cannot work for more than 4 hours without a one-hour break, for more than 2 hours on any school day a or Sunday before 7a.m. or after 7am for more than one hour before school starts, for more than 12 hours in any school week

کسی بھی دن میں لگا تار چار گھنٹے بغیر ایک گھنٹے کی بریک کے کام نہیں کر سکتے اور سکول والے دن دو گھنٹے سے زیادہ کام نہیں کر سکتے سنڈے کے دن سات بجے سے پہلے کام نہیں کر سکتے اور سکول کے دنوں میں سات بجے سے پہلے یا بعد میں ایک گھنٹے سے زیادہ کام نہیں کر سکتے۔ اور پورے ہفتے میں بارہ گھنٹوں سے زیادہ کام نہیں کر سکتے۔

15 and 16-year-olds can work slightly more hours than 14-year-olds on a weekday when they are not at school, on Saturdays and in school holidays

15-16 سال کے بچے 14 سال کی نسبت زیادہ کام کر سکتے ہیں بشرطکہ سکول نہ ہو

The local authority has a duty to check that the law is obeyed. if it believes that a young person is working illegally, it can order that the young person is no longer employed.

لوکل اتھارٹی کی ڈیوٹی ہے کہ قانون کے خلاف فرضی نہ ہو اگر انہیں پتہ چلے تو اس کو دوبارہ نوکری نہیں کرنے دی جائیگی

84

Chapter 6 Practice Test

(1) If you are late for work,
  A. Your employer can give you a warning, then dismiss you if you are late again
  B. Your employer can dismiss you immediately
  C. Your employer cannot dismiss you because trade unions would protest
  D. Your employer can go to the Employment Tribunal and have you dismissed

(2) Jobseeker's Allowance is currently available to
  A. Men and women capable of working, available for work and trying to find work, unless they reached the state pension age
  B. Men and women aged at least 18, capable of working, available for work and trying to find work, unless they reached the state pension age
  C. Men and women capable of working, available for work and trying to find work
  D. Anybody who is unemployed

(3) If you are an adult and have been unemployed for one year and a half, you
  A. Lose your right to benefits
  B. Get reduced benefits
  C. Are usually required to join New Deal
  D. Lose your work permit

(4) British Citizens can work in any country that is a member of the
  A. Council of Europe
  B. Commonwealth
  C. NATO
  D. European Economic Area

(5) Who is entitled to maternity leave?
  A. Women, must have been employed for at least 6 months.
  B. Women and men, who have been employed for at least 26 weeks.
  C. Women with no employment length requirements and men after 26 weeks.
  D. Women, no minimum previous employment length.

(6) Children under 14 can work
  A. In any areas, provided they have a special licence
  B. Delivering milk
  C. In performing, modeling, sport and agriculture
  D. For two weeks every year

(7) While considering your application, an employer
  A. Can do a criminal record check without your knowledge
  B. Can do a criminal record check with your permission
  C. Can do a criminal record check without your permission if the job involves working with children or vulnerable people
  D. Cannot do a criminal record check in no circumstances

(8) Information about volunteering opportunities can be found
  A. At your local library
  B. At Jobcentre Plus
  C. At Citizen's Advice Bureau
  D. At Business Link

(9) Where can you go for advice and help in finding and applying for a job as well as claiming benefits?
  A. Jobcentre Plus
  B. Home Office
  C. Employment Agency
  D. NARIC

(10) National Academic Recognition Information Centre
  A. Helps you apply for a job in the UK
  B. Analyzes foreign diplomas and compares them to the British qualifications
  C. Helps you claim your Jobseekers' Allowance
  D. Tells you whether you are allowed to work.

(11) What is a CV?
  A. Covering Voucher, explains why you are the most suitable person for the job
  B. Community Volunteer, a title that gives you priority when you apply for a job
  C. Curriculum Vitae, gives specific details on your education, qualifications, previous employment, skills and interests
  D. Criminal Verification, needed if the job involves working with children

Chapter 6

(12) Learndirect offers
A. comparison of foreign qualifications to the British ones
B. assistance with claiming benefits
C. volunteering opportunities
D. online training courses

(13) Referees
A. Have to be present at the job interview with you
B. Need to check with the Home Office if they are eligible to be referees
C. Usually have to paid for their reports
D. Cannot be family members or personal friends

(14) You may not be refused work if you
A. Don't have enough experience
B. Have a criminal record
C. Are handicapped
D. Don't have the relevant qualification

(15) Discrimination laws do not apply if you
A. Are in performing, modelling, sport and agriculture
B. Are working for someone in their own home
C. Are working with children or vulnerable people
D. Lied about your qualifications

(16) If a woman touches a male coworker inappropriately, or makes sexual demands
A. He should tell a friend and ask the woman to stop, keep a written record of what happened, and report her to the employer if she persists
B. He should treat her in a way that is rude, hostile, degrading and humiliating
C. He should make comments about the way she looks
D. He should seek advice from the Equal Opportunities Commission

(17) The minimum wage your employer may pay you depends on your
A. Age   B. Sex
C. Qualifications   D. Status in UK

(18) If your employer asks you to work more hours than the amount mentioned in your contract,
A. You must refuse as it is not legal to work more than agreed upon in the contract
B. You can accept or refuse
C. You should accept, otherwise you may lose your job
D. You should ask him or her to stop, and keep a written record of what happened

(19) Your employer should give you a pay slip or a similar written statement
A. Once a year, stating all the payments made to you
B. At the end of your employment
C. Each time you are paid
D. Once a week, usually on the same week day

(20) If you are self-employed,
A. Tax is automatically taken from your account by the bank or the building society
B. You don't have to pay taxes, if you don't use government services such as roads and police
C. You should only pay Class 4 national insurance contributions, but no tax
D. You need to pay your own tax

86

(21) National Insurance (NI) contributions should be paid by
A. Everybody in the UK
B. Everybody in the UK who wishes to be eligible for certain benefits, such as Jobseeker's Allowance or Maternity Pay
C. Everybody with a valid work permit in the UK
D. Everybody in the UK who is in paid work

(22) A National Insurance Number can be obtained through
A. Home Office
B. Learn Direct
C. Jobcentre plus or a local Social Security office
D. BusinessLink

(23) You will get a state Pension at 60,
A. If you are a man
B. If you are a woman and if you paid enough NI contributions
C. If you are a woman
D. If you are a man and paid enough NI contributions

(24) Trade unions are
A. Organisations that aim to improve the pay and working conditions of their members
B. Organisations that aim to improve the pay and working conditions of all workers in the UK
C. Organisations that assist you with maternity issues and give advice on contraception
D. Companies specialized in international trade

(25) If you are late for work,
A. Your employer can give you a warning, then dismiss you if you are late again
B. Your employer can dismiss you immediately
C. Your employer cannot dismiss you because trade unions would protest
D. Your employer can go to the Employment Tribunal and have you dismissed

(26) Jobseeker's Allowance is currently available to
A. Men and women capable of working, available for work and trying to find work, unless they reached the state pension age
B. Men and women aged at least 18, capable of working, available for work and tryin g to find work, unless they reached the state pension age
C. Men and women capable of working, available for work and trying to find work
D. Anybody who is unemployed

(27) If you are an adult and have been unemployed for one year and a half, you
A. Lose your right to benefits
B. Get reduced benefits
C. Are usually required to join New Deal
D. Lose your work permit

(28) British Citizens can work in any country that is a member of the
A. Council of Europe
B. Commonwealth
C. NATO
D. European Economic Area

(29) Who is entitled to maternity leave?
A. Women, must have been employed for at least 6 months.
B. Women and men, who have been employed for at least 26 weeks.
C. Women with no employment length requirements and men after 26 weeks.
D. Women, no minimum previous employment length

(30) Children under 14 can work
A. In any areas, provided they have a special licence
B. Delivering milk
C. In performing, modeling, sport and agriculture
D. For two weeks every year

Chapter 6

(31) While considering your application, an employer can
   A. Can do a criminal record check without your knowledge
   B. Can do a criminal record check with your permission
   C. Can do a criminal record check without your permission if the job involves working with children or vulnerable people
   D. Cannot do a criminal record check in no circumstances

(32) Information about volunteering opportunities can be found
   A. At your local library   B. At Jobcentre Plus
   C. At Citizen's Advice Bureau   D. At Business Link

33) In England careers advice for children 14 and over is available from Connexions. Is this statement true or false?
   A True   B False

34 Select the correct statement
   A It is illegal to discriminate against someone for employment in any circumstances
   B Discrimination is not against the law when the job involves working for someone in their own home

35 At what age can men get a state pension?
   A 55 years old B 60 years old C 65 years old D ^0 years old

36 Select the correct statement
   A You must be at least 18 years old to be eligible for a Young Person's Bridging Allowance
   B Yon must be 16 or 17 years old to be eligible for a Young Person's Bridging Allowance

37 What is the minimum age required to drive a car?
   A 16 years old B 17 years old   C 18 years old   D 21 years old

38 Which of these statements is correct?
   A An identity card is the only document that can be used to prove your identity
   B A driving licence or a recent phone bill may be used to prove your identity

39 What does the Family Planning Association provide advice on? Select two options from below
   A Sexual heath   B Contraception
   C Family values   D Ambulance services

40 Parents are not allowed to sit on a school's governing body. Is this statement true or false?
   A True   B False

(41) By law, men and women who do the same job should receive equal pay. Is this statement true or false?
   A True B False

(42) Al what age can women get a state pension?
   A 55 years old B 60 years old
   C 65 years old D 70 years old

(43) which of the following statements is correct?
   A As soon as you become self-employed you should register yourself for National Insurance and tax by contacting HM Revenue and Customs
   B Is it necessary to contact the HM Revenue and Customs when you become self-employed

44 What is the maximum number of hours that a child can work on a school day or Sunday?
   A Eight hours   B Four hours
   C Six hours   D Two hours

45 At what age do children in England go to secondary school?
   A 11   B 12   C 15   D 9

46 Within what period of time must a baby be registered with the Registrar of Births, Marriages and Deaths?
   A One week   B Six months   C Six weeks   D Twelve months

47 How many days a year must a school open?
   A 100 days   B 150 days   C 190 days   D 365 days

48 It is illegal for a child to work for more than one hour ora Bchool starts. Is this statement true or false?
   A True   B False

49 Where can you apply for a National Insurance ? Select two options from below
   A Any Jobcentre Plus branch
   B your local Social Security Office
   C your local library   D your cal council or town hall

50 British citizens require a work permit before they can work in any country that is a member of the European Economic Area.
   A True   B False

51 What is the financial help called that is available to young >ple from low income families who leave school early?
   A After School Allowance
   B Education Maintenance Allowance
   C Housing Benefit
   D School Leaver's Payment

52 in Northern Ireland, it is legal to discriminate on grounds of religious belief or political opinion. Is this statement true or false?
   A True   B False

53 For what reason could you be immediately dismissed from your job?
   A because of serious misconduct   B because of your age
   C because of your religious beliefs   D because of your sexuality

54 What is the minimum number of weeks maternity leave that i women are entitled to?
   A 11 weeks   B 16 weeks   C 21 weeks   D 26 weeks

1A 2C 3C 4D   5D   6C   7C 8C 9A 10B 11C 12D 13D 14C   15B 16A 17A 18B 19C
20D 21D   22C 23B   24A 25A 26C 27C 28D 29D 30C 31C 32 C 33 A 34 B 35C 36B
37B   38B 39 B 40 B 41 A 42 B 43 B 44D 45A   46 C 47 C 48 A 49A 50B   51B
52A 53A 54D

Time line of British History edited by Rehan Afzal

Church of England is a Protestant church and has existed since the Reformation in the 1530s.

Guy Fawkes Night 5 November, is an occasion when people in Great Britain set off fireworks at home or in special displays. The origin of this celebration was an event in 1605, when a group of Catholics led by Guy Fawkes failed in their plan to kill the Protestant king.

16th and 18th centuries, Huguenots (French Protestants) came to Britain to 16th and 18th centuries Huguenots escape religious persecution in France.

A census has been taken every ten years since 1801, except during the Second World War. The next census will take place in 2011.

mid-1840s there was a terrible famine
mid 1840 Ireland and many Irish people migrated to Britain
Until 1857, a married woman had no right to divorce her husband
Until 1882, when a woman got married, her earnings, property and money automatically belonged to her husband.

1880 to 1910, A large number of Jewish people came to Britain to escape racist attacks (called 'pogroms'

in 1918,women over the age of 30 were only given the right to vote and to stand for election to Parliament

In 1918 the first world war ended.
1928 that women won the right to vote at 21, at the same age as men.
The United Kingdom has had a fully democratic system since 1928.

After the Second World War (1939-45), there was a huge task of rebuilding Britain

1948, people from the West Indies were also invited to come to work
The Council of Europe was created in 1949 and the UK was one of the founder members

1950s, there was still a shortage of labour in the UK
The Queen has reigned since her father's death in 1952.

The European Union (EU), originally six called the European Economic Community(EEC), was set up by Western European countries on 25 March 1957.
Until 1958 all peers were hereditary.

Since 1958 the Prime Minister has had the power to appoint peers just for their own lifetime

1960s the government passed new laws to restrict immigration to Britain and 1960 people migrating in these areas fell.

The present voting age of 18 was set in 1969,

Trouble broke in 1969 in Northern Ireland and caused assembly suspension

During the 1960s and 1970s there was increasing pressure from women for equal rights. Parliament passed new laws giving women the right to equal pay and prohibiting employers from discriminating against women

since 1971 the population has grown 7.7% and growth has been faster in more recent years.

The UK decided not to join this group and only became part of the European Union in 1973.

1980s the largest immigrant groups came from the United States, Australia, South Africa, and New Zealand.

Early 1990s, groups of people from the former Soviet Union came to Britain looking for a new and safer way of life.

Since 1994 there has been a global rise in mass migration for both political and economic.

In 19th-century Britain, families were usually large and in many poorer homes men, women and children all contributed for income

In the late 19th and early 20th centuries, an increasing number of women campaigned and demonstrated for greater rights and, in particular, the right to vote. They became known as 'Suffragettes'.

In the 2001 general election, however only 1 in 5 first - time voters used their vote

In January 2002 twelve European Union (EU) states adopted the euro as their common currency.

In 2003 a survey of young people in England and Wales showed that they believe the five most important issues in Britain were crime ,drugs , war/ terrorism, racism and health.

In 2004 ten new member countries joined the EU, with a further two in 2006 making a total of 27 member countries

Since 2004 from the new East European member states of the European Union.

Since 2005, it is now possible for the Lord Chancellor to sit in the Commons

In Northern Ireland water is currently (2006) included in the domestic rates,

Practice Exam-1

1. What is the name of the election held to replace an MP who has died or resigned between general elections?
Mark one answer
A by-election
A mid-term election
TO A snap election

2. Is this statement TRUE or FALSE?
Seats in the European Parliament are allocated to each party in proportion to the total number of votes it has won in the election.
A True   B False

3. Which statement is true?
Most local authorities provide housing for rent.
You cannot rent accommodation from a local authority.

4. Which statement is correct?
Mark one answer
A There are no penalties for being drunk in public.
B Penalties to try to reduce binge-drinking include on-the-spot fines for being drunk in public.

5. If you want to buy a home, where is usually the best place to start?
Mark one answer
A An estate agent   B A post office
C A solicitor   D A newspaper
At what age can young people leave school?
Mark one answer
A 17   B 16   C 18   D 15

6. Which statement is correct?
A A by-election is held when an MP is standing for Parliament for the last time.
B by-election is held in the constituency of an MP

7. who dies or resigns.
When was the United Nations (UN) set up?
Mark one answer
A After the Second World War
B 1957
C 1949
D 2004

92

8 When did the UK join the European Union?
A 1973   B 2004   C 1957   D 1949

Is this statement TRUE or FALSE?
Young people in the UK are not interested in Politics
A True B False

9 How many national regions are there within the United Kingdom?
Mark one answer
A 5   B 6   C 4   D 10

10 Which statement is correct?
A There are almost 15 million children and young people up to the age of 19 in the UK population.
B There are almost 20 million children and young

11 people up to the age of 19 in the UK population. What is the estimated number of young people who have part-time jobs while they are still at school?
Mark one answer
A 500,000   B 1 million   C 2 million   D 3 million

12 Who is the patron saint of Wales?
Mark one answer
A St David B St Andrew C St George D St Patrick

13 Which statement is correct?
Mark one answer
A As well as the State Pension, many people receive an occupational pension through their work, and some also receive a personal pension.
B The state pension is the only pension scheme available.

14 How many independent schools are there in the UK? Mark one answer
A About 5,000   B About 2,500   C About 25,000   D About 500

Practice Exam-1

15 Who did the government invite to help rebuild ' Britain in 1945?
Mark one answer
A Workers from Ireland and other parts of Europe
B Workers from America and Australia
C Workers from the Caribbean
D Workers from Asia

16 Which areas of work are traditionally female? Mark one answer
A Health care, teaching, secretarial and retail work
B Farming, fishing, coal-mining and diving
C Law- polltics' arm@d forces and policing
D Engineering, science, building and finance

17 Is this statement TRUE or FALSE?
Children in the UK aged between 5 and 16 do not have to go to school if they don't want to.
A True B False

18 "Which ONE of these two statements is correct
A Christmas is only celebrated by Christians.
B Most people celebrate Christmas.

19 Who can get a free or discounted TV licence?
Mark one answer
A You can get a free TV licence if your landlord has a licence. If you watch TV for fewer than 10 hours a week you can get a 50 discount.
B People aged 75 and over can get a free TV
A licence. Blind people can get a 50 discount.
C People aged 65 and over can get a free TV Licence. A family with children under 12 can get a 25% discount.

20 (Which statement TRUE or FALSE? The Speaker represents Parliament at official occasions.
A TRUE   B FALSE

21 Which statement is correct?
A Before a general election top civil servants prepare their resignation letters in case the government changes.
B Before a general election top civil servants study the Opposition party policies closely in case they need to be ready to serve a new government

(22) Mortgage is
A. A special loan from a bank or a building society, used to pay for a home
B. A check on the house done by a surveyor
C. The name of the deposit left to the owner at the beginning of tenancy
D. The name of a real estate purchase agreement in Scotland

(23) You are more likely to obtain council housing if you
A. Are self-employed B. Are unemployed
C. Have a local connection D. Are homeless, have children or chronic ill health

(24) Lease is
A. The benefit available to homeless
B. An ownership scheme ran by Housing Associations
C. The list of furniture or fittings in the property
D. The document that you sign when you rent a house or flat

```
1A  2B  3C  4B  5A  6A  7B  8C  9C  10A
11C  12D  13A  14B  15A  16A  17B  18B  19B
20B  21B  22A  23D  24D
```

Practice Exam-2

Is this statement true or false?
1 There are very few places for a mother to take a child who is too young for school?
    A True   B False

2 What proportion of UK population is of non white (Asian/Asian British, Black/ Black British,
Chinese and mixed) descent? Mark one answer
    A 32.6% B 2.7% C 8.3% D 5.1%

3 How can the public listen to debates in the parliament
Mark one answer
    A There are listening booths outside parliament
    B The public are not permitted to enter the parliament
    C Anyone can sit with MPs or peers
    D There are public galleries in the house of commons and the house of lords

4 Is this statement true or false?
All members of parliament (MPs) belong to a political party.
    A True   B False

5 When is Guy Fawkes' Night?
    A 31st October   B 25th December
    C 5th November   D 11 November

6 Is this statement true or false?
There are no laws about how old children must be before they can work
    A True   B False

7 England and Wales have four holidays other tan bank holidays.
    A April Fool's Day ,Queen's Birth day, Hallowe'en and Guy Fawkes' Night
    B New Year's Day, Good Friday, Christmas Day, and Boxing Day
    C St. Valentine's Day, April Fool's Day, Harvest Festival and Remembrance Day
    D St. David's day, St.Patrick's day, st.George's Day and St.Andrew's Day

8 What is a shared ownership scheme?
Mark one answer
    A A way to buy a house or flat in stages, with the help of a housing association
    B A way to buy a house or flat with other people
    C A way to buy a flat or house with the help of a local authority
    D A way to sell part of your house or flat to someone else without having to pay any tax on the money.

9 Is this statement true or false
The house of lord is more independent of the government than the house of commons.
A True   B False

10 Which statement is correct ?
A Discrimination against someone looking for accommodation because of race, sex, nationality, ethnic group or disability is always illegal.
B In some situations, discrimination against someone looking for accommodation because of race, sex, nationality, ethnic group or disability Can be legal.

11 How can constituents contact an elected member?
Mark two answers
A In person at their home
B Often, in person at a local surgery
C By phone at their home
D By letter or phone at their constituency office or parliamentary office

12 When might you receive redundancy pay?
A If the company that you work for dismisses you because it cannot afford to employ you, or it no longer needs someone to do your job, you may be entitled to redundancy pay.
B If the company that you work for wants to dismisses you because it cannot afford to employ you, or it no longer needs someone to do your job, it does not have to pay you any compensation.

13 Why did the government encourage workers to come to Britain in 1945?
Mark one answer
A To do the job that British people didn't want to do
B To help in the huge task of rebuilding Britain after
C To make the British society more multi-ethnic
D To thanks the countries which had helped Britain during the war

14 What must everyone in a private vehicle wear?
A A life jacket   B A crash helmet
C A seat belt D An identification badge

15 Which one of these two statements is correct?
A People living in Scotland, Wales and Northern Ireland have their own language
B No one speaks Gaelic, Welsh, or Irish Gaelic today

16 Who has to pay council tax?
A Everyone who is the owner or tenant of property
B All landlord   C Everyone who is eligible to vote
D All property -owners

97

Practice Exam-2

1 Is this statement True or False?
The role of judiciary in interpreting the law has become more important in recent years because judges now have the task of applying the Human Rights Act.
A True   B False

2 Which statement is correct?
Mark one answer.
A Two-third of young people go on to higher education in a college or university
B One-quarter of young people go on to higher education or university
C One-half of young people go on to higher education or university
D One-third of young people go on higher education or university.

3 Which statement is correct?
A You can buy or change foreign currency at banks, large post offices, building societies and exchange shops or bureau de change.
B you have to go to the embassy of a country to buy or change its currency.

4 Is this statement True or False?
There is no minimum wage in the UK.
A True   B False

5 In which elections is proportional representation used?
A In elections to the Westminster Parliament
B in election to the Welsh Assembly, Scottish parliament, Northern Irel and Assembly and the European Parliament

6 Is this statement True or False?
Women were given equal rights with men in 1928.
A True   B False

7 Among the school-age population, do girls or boys smoke most?
A Girls   B Boys

8 Who chooses the Archbishop of Canterbury?
Mark two answers
A The monarch (king or queen)   C The prime minister and c a committee appointed by the church of England
D The last Archbishop of Canterbury   B The pope

9 Is this statement True or False?
Your local education authority or the Citizens' Advice Bureau can advise you on getting help with the costs of sending your child to state secondary school.
A True   B False

10 What is the estimated number of young people who have part-time jobs while they are still at school ?
    Mark one answer
A 2 million   B 1 million   C   500,000   D   3 million

11 Which statement is correct?
A Elected members do not have to represent their constituents.
B All elected members have a duty to serve and represent their constituents

12 Which statement is correct?
A Citizenship is not taught at school.
B Most children study Citizenship at school.

98

17 Is this statement true or false?
EU laws have made a great difference to people's rights in the UK.
    A True   B False

18 Is this statement true or false?
Children are in more danger now of being attacked by strangers than in the past
    A True   B False

19 What school subject helps children to get involved in community and charity activities
Mark one answer
    A Social Studies   B Economics
    C Citizenship   D Politics

20 Who can stand for public office in the UK?
Mark one answer
    A Most citizens of the EU, UK , Irish Republic and commonwealth aged 18or older
    B Most citizens of the UK, Irish Republic and commonwealth aged 18 or older
    C Anyone with a family connection with the UK
    D Anyone resident in the UK and aged 18 or older

21 The average hourly rate of pay for men is higher than for women paid - how much less are women paid?
    A 20%   B 1%   C 7%   D 16%

22 Why was the European Union created?
Mark one answer
    A To reduce the number of languages spoken in Europe
    B To make another war in Europe less likely
    C To help trade between the member countries
    D To create a European superpower

23 Which statement is correct?
    A The law says that parents are responsible for deciding whether their children can work, what work they can do an how many hours they can work
    B there are laws about the usual minimum age at which children work they can do how many hours they can work

24 Is this statement true or false?
Young people are not allowed to buy alcohol until they are 18.
    A True   B False

    1B 2C 3D 4B 5C 6B 7B 8B 9B 10B
    11BD 12A 13B 14C 15A 16A 17A 18B 19C
    20D 21A 22B 23B 24A

1 Is this statement True or False?
The role of judiciary in interpreting the law has become more important in recent years because judges now have the task of applying the Human Rights Act.
    A True   B False

2 Which statement is correct? Mark one answer.
    A Two-third of young people go on to higher education in a college or university
    B One-quarter of young people go on to higher education or university
    C One-half of young people go on to higher education or university
    D One-third of young people go on higher education or university.

3 Which statement is correct?
    A You can buy or change foreign currency at banks, large post offices, building societies and exchange shops or bureau de change.
    B you have to go to the embassy of a country to buy or change its currency.

4 Is this statement True or False?
There is no minimum wage in the UK.
    A True   B False

5 In which elections is proportional representation used?
    A In elections to the Westminster Parliament
    B in election to the Welsh Assembly, Scottish parliament, Northern Ireland Assembly and the European Parliament

6 Is this statement True or False?
Women were given equal rights with men in 1928.
    A True   B False

7 Among the school-age population, do girls or boys smoke most?
    A Girls   B Boys

8 Who chooses the Archbishop of Canterbury?
Mark two answers
    A The monarch (king or queen)   D The last Archbishop of Canterbury
    B The Pope C The prime minister and CA committee appointed by the church of England

9 Is this statement True or False?
Your local education authority or the Citizens' Advice Bureau can advise you on getting help with the costs of sending your child to state secondary school.
    A True   B False

10 What is the estimated number of young people who have part-time jobs while they are still at school ? Mark one answer
    A 2 million   B 1 million C 500,000   D 3 million

11 Which statement is correct?
    A Elected members do not have to represent their constituents.
    B All elected members have a duty to serve and represent their constituents

12 Which statement is correct?
    A Citizenship is not taught at school.
    B Most children study Citizenship at school.

13 Which groups of people have come to Britain in the past to escape religious persecution.
Mark two answers
A West Indies B Jews   C Irish people D Huguenots (French Protestants)
Mark one answer
A Wales B Scotland C Engalnd D   Northern Ireland

14 Is this statement True or False?
You can get information about Islamic (Sharia) mortgages from some banks
A True   B False

15   In Government, what do the initials PM stand for? Mark one answer
A Prime Minister   B Presidential Minister
C Principal Minister   D Prime Minister

16 How often do EU countries elect members to sit in the European Parliament?
Mark one answer
A Every 5 years   B Every 4 years
C Every year   D every 3 years

17   What is the longest distance on the UK mainland?   Mark one answer
A   about 1,600 miles (about 2,574 kilometers)
B   about 2,000 miles (about 3,218 kilometers)
C   about 740 miles (about 1,191 kilometers)
D   about 870 miles (about 1,400 kilometers)

18 Is this statement True or False?
The procedure for buying a home is different in Scotland from the rest of the UK
A True   B False

19 Which statement is correct?
A EU citizens who are resident in the UK can vote in all UK public elections
B EU citizens who are resident in the UK ca vote in all UK public elections except national parliamentary elections.

20 Is this statement true or false?
If you receive Housing Benefit, this may include water rates.
    A True   B False

21 What sport is played at the cup final ?
Mark one answer
A Football B Tennis C Rugby D Cricket

22 Which statements is correct?
A In many communities, young people often move out of their family home when they become adults
B It is very uncommon for young people to move out of their family home when they become adults.

23 Is this statement true or false?
A pressure or lobby group tries to influence government policy.
A True   B False

(24) Advice on contraception is available from
A. the National Childbirth Trust   B. Citizens Advice Bureau
C. the Family Planning Association (FPA)   D. CRB or Disclosure Scotland

1A 2D 3A 4B 5B 6A 7A 8AC 9A 10A
11B 12B 13 BD 14C 15A 16A 17A 18D 19A
20B 21A 22A 23A 24C